LIVING BEYOND 90

"At the Canadian National Table Tennis Championships In 1962, a precision-guided orange peel hit Dean square in the back of the head. Dean turned to see where it came from and saw the angelic, smiling face of Helga, who he had met not long before. Dean and Helga were soon to marry. Being very spiritual beings, Dean and I would call that precision-guided peel a divinely inspired event. Meant to be. Sure, Helga was a great athlete, but just a little high or to the right or left and perhaps Dean's life journey is changed forever. As Dean puts it, 'Helga is the mate that fate had me created for.'

"In this beautifully written book, you'll see how, as Dean puts it, 'every piece in my puzzle, guided by divine inspiration, was fitting together perfectly.' My goodness, Babe Ruth is even a part of this amazing puzzle—along with some of the greatest ping-pong (table tennis) players of their era, like Dick Miles and Marty Reisman, etc., etc., and basketball legend Christian Laettner (also a very good ping-pong player). Like Dean, I believe ping-pong is like life itself in all its ebbs and flows and spins and curves and chops you must deal with that come at you at various speeds. That said, Dean shares in the book how nearly every business client since the late 1960s was connected to table tennis—and that continued for more than forty years. Dean believes, as I do, that certain things in life are destined. 'Destiny can't be denied,' but you have to have the courage to, as Dean puts it, 'Just show up.'"

—Adoni Maropis, dear friend of angels Dean and Helga Johnson

"It is my honor and a blessing to write this for my dearest friend, Dean. We have been part of each other's lives for the past forty-five-plus years. My story: Back in 1977, when I was a nineteen-year-old draftsman at Sier Bath Gear in North Bergen, NJ, we used real pencils to draw on what was called vellum. I distinctly remember this nice, friendly guy called Dean. I didn't know him, but he oversaw our marketing and printed materials, and he would come by to check to see if I needed more paper for my drawings.

"At the time, I had a very significant to me but poor-quality, wrinkled quote from Albert Einstein pinned to my wall. Dean asked if he could look at it and take a photocopy for himself. The following week, Dean dropped off this beautiful typeset copy of that quote. This was long before computers, and back then, things needed to be typeset. I still have that quote printed by Dean, and it's hung in every office I ever had during the past forty-five years.

"Fast-forward through a lifetime of jobs, careers, marriage, kids, grandkids, weddings, and funerals, and I am still blessed to have Dean in my life. What's most important is having full confidence that Dean will ALWAYS be in my life because life goes on. Life is just about love. We're here for a short while in order to learn to love. When we've learned that lesson, God allows us to graduate, and we get to move to the second floor. That's it; that's what life is all about. We both once worked for a guy that said, 'If you live long enough, you get to see how it all worked out.' How right he was.

"My single greatest lesson from Dean was to take one day at a time. As I was struggling through night school for eleven years, Dean would say, "Marcelo, just get through today; don't worry about tomorrow." Years later I would learn that most of Dean's most important quotes came from the Bible.

"Over the years, my conversations with Dean broached many

subjects, but the one we discussed most was the subject of God. Is He real? What does He expect from us? How do we please Him? Dean is a true believer, and we spent countless days discussing the meaning of life and 'Godwinks.'

"Although I'm now in my sixties and Dean is beyond ninety, we still discuss these things and more. This latest book by Dean is about his story and how God sends different people throughout our life to teach us valuable lessons. To this I say, ninety more years, Dean!"

—Marcelo

"Oh, Dean, what an amazing book! So grateful for having met you, and now reading these stories coming to us from a span of almost a century is such a treat! Thank you for taking us on a journey of your life!"

—Ioanna Papadimitriou

Living Beyond 90: How God Led 50 Friends of Mine to Pave a Path for Me Beyond the 90s
by Dean Johnson

Published as a special edition legacy book by

 köehlerbooks™

3705 Shore Drive
Virginia Beach, VA 23455
800-435-4811
www.koehlerbooks.com

DEAN JOHNSON

LIVING
BEYOND
90

How God Led 50 Friends of Mine
to Pave a Path for Me Beyond the 90s

VIRGINIA BEACH
CAPE CHARLES

TABLE OF CONTENTS

DISCLAIMER:

THERE ARE A few amazing pieces of writing out there documenting the lives of table tennis pros. I am lucky enough to have interacted with some of these wonderful people throughout my life. Along with my personal accounts—how I've made it this far, *ninety years old*—I draw on a few published works that outline the biographies of some of my closest friends. I do hope you enjoy.

Parts of this book are featured on the USA Table Tennis Nationals Virginia Beach Facebook page, written by the author, posted in 2018 (all edited for clarity).

INTRODUCTION

ONE SLEEPLESS NIGHT, a question occurred to me. How did I get to be ninety? Where did the years go? Who were the people and what were the events that brought me to where I am at this moment? I'm going to share with you a series of short stories, all of which are true and intimately linked by what I believe to be a collection of *divinely inspired* people and events, and how these events lead from the day of my birth to this moment in time.

I had little or no control over the people or events I describe here, with very few exceptions. They are, I believe, examples of how God's Grace worked in my life.

The answer to this question started more than 120 years ago

when a young couple named Anna and Fred Johnson, recent immigrants from Scandinavia, decided to move from New York, where they lived and were married in 1898, to Passaic, New Jersey.

From the moment they got here (Anna immigrated in 1892, and Fred followed in 1897), they both worked hard; Fred drove a team of horses for a local winery and worked as a gardener. Anna Marie worked as a housekeeper and chef for a wealthy New York family named Green.

Anna Marie was a beauty. Judging by a collection of photos, which I inherited from her, she may have also spent some time working as a fashion model in New York City.

In 1903, from the money this couple was able to save, they bought a six-acre plot on Bloomfield Avenue in Clifton, New Jersey, on which they built a small house. In this house, which was not much larger than a garage by today's standards, four of their children were born. In 1909, they built another, larger home (photo on page 6) on the lot where two more children were born. The small house was then converted into a garage.

They had another life-altering story of relocation. In the early-1920s, a couple named Mary and Michael Donohue, living in Garfield, New Jersey, had a beautiful, brick, three-story, four-bedroom home built three miles to the south on the very same Bloomfield Avenue in Clifton. The home they built was just a block and a half north of the Johnson home.

So, this decision by Michael and Mary Donohue marked the beginning of an incredible story about how—by what I believe to be a series of *divinely inspired* events—this relocation by the Donohue's determined the path of my life.

The proximity of these homes in the 1930s and the interaction of the two families living there—the Donohue's and the Johnson's—had an enormous impact on the destiny of both of these families for generations to come. The proximity of this home to the Donohue's home built in 1921 was what led to the connection and the eventual marriage of my parents, Dean Johnson and Helen Donohue.

So, my life really began with a long series of coincidental, magical, unbroken, continuous links spanning more than 100 years—the proximity of this Donohue move, just a block and a half from the Johnson's, leading to one of the three Donohue girls (Helen) and one of the six Johnson boys (Dean, my father) getting together. They were married in April 1931. I was born in January 1932, and thus began what I believe to be the *divinely inspired* story of my life and how I was guided to where I am at this moment.

MARY & MICHAEL DONOHUE

WHATEVER LED TO that early-1920s decision by Mary and Michael Donohue, to build a new home on Bloomfield Avenue in Clifton, marked the beginning of an incredible story about how a series of *divinely inspired* events, starting with this relocation, determined the path of my life over the next ninety years.

The Donohues had two children, a girl and a boy—Helen and John. Mary had two other children—Lillian and Mae—by a previous marriage to William Flynn.

Helen, my mother, was ten years old at the time the Donohues moved from Garfield to Clifton. Michael, along with two of

4

his brothers, James and Patrick, became very wealthy during prohibition.

In addition to owning speakeasies, Michael was a professional boxer and boxing promoter.

Another of Michael's brothers, Thomas, was City Clerk of nearby Passaic. Michael had a sister named Helen and two brothers named John and Joseph.

ANNA MARIE & FRED JOHNSON

WHEN I WAS born in January 1932, the country was in the depths of the Depression. The company for whom my father was working in 1931, Fokker Aircraft in Teterboro, New Jersey, was absorbed by the Aircraft Division of General Motors in Baltimore, so my parents (my mother, pregnant with me at the time) relocated to a row house in Baltimore. Not long after we arrived in Baltimore, my grandmother Anna began traveling back and forth by train from Clifton, New Jersey, to Baltimore, to help her twenty-year-old daughter-in-law care for me, my father,

Anna's thirty-two-year-old son LeRoy, and a boarder my parents took in to help pay the rent. But my mother found life too difficult in Baltimore, so in November 1933, she and I moved back to Clifton to live with her parents—the Donohue's—on Bloomfield Avenue.

With that relocation, my mother and I lived in relative comfort. The Donohue's, by standards of the '30s, were wealthy. But my father lost his job with Fokker, and he began moving from job to job—from vacuum cleaner salesman to magazine truck driver to "counter" man at one of the Donohue's road-stands in Union, New Jersey.

These jobs, according to my mother, were among the more than twenty my father held during his career.

We lived with the Donohue's until November 1, 1934, at which time Mom and Dad reconciled and we moved to a small apartment on Broadway in Passaic until April 1, 1935.

HELEN & JOHN DONOHUE

MY GRANDMOTHER DONOHUE was a longtime friend of a woman named Eliza Murray Coates. Eliza and her family lived just a block and a half down Scoles Avenue from the Donohues.

When my grandmother Donohue told Eliza that her daughter was looking for a place to rent, Eliza told her that a house next to hers on Scoles Avenue was available.

My mother contacted the owner, Jennie Brown, about availability and price; Mrs. Brown was asking $25/month. My mother and father agreed to her terms, and on April 1, 1935, we all moved to a modest rental at 87 Scoles Avenue in Clifton—next door to the Coates family! My mother was very proud of her little "bungalow." This relocation, clearly *divinely inspired*, was to have a profound impact on the Johnson family for generations to come!

Helen Donohue, my mother, was born on May 4, 1911, in Passaic, New Jersey. Her brother, John, was born on April 4, 1913, in Garfield. All their lives, they were very close; they supported each other. I was blessed to have Helen for a mother and John for an uncle.

I think my mother was a saint for the way she handled the many hardships she faced in her marriage. She was raised in a well-to-do family but from the time she was married at twenty until she died at seventy-nine, her life was a constant challenge. Yet she handled it with patience and grace and prayer.

Every night, she would pray with me, "Now I lay me down to sleep. I pray the Lord my soul to keep. If I should die before I wake, I pray the Lord my soul to take." That was followed by a blessing for every family member. *God bless Gammy and Pop. God bless Gram and Mike. God bless Uncle John*—and so it would go until every family member was blessed. Then she would say to me, "Now let's be quiet and listen to God." I didn't know what she meant then; but I know now. It's called meditation. The last words Ma said to me before she died were "Jesus suffered. Why shouldn't I?"

John and Helen died within five weeks of each other in June and July 1990.

As a youth, John Donohue had "Hollywood" good looks.

As an athlete, he was so talented he might have been a major-league baseball player. As a singer, he had such a good voice, he might have been a crooner—better than Crosby, as good as Sinatra.

As John Greenleaf Whittier once wrote, "*For of all sad words of tongue or pen, the saddest are these, 'It might have been."*

"I had it too good and was just too lazy, Bob. I didn't use the gifts I was given," he once confessed to me. (He called me Bob, after my middle name, just like my mother. With two Deans in the house [my father too], it was easier.)

Uncle John taught me valuable lessons through the example of his life. But not all the examples were good.

JIMMY DONOHUE & BABE RUTH

IN MY TEENS, I was impressed and inspired by my granduncle Jimmy Donohue.

Jimmy started in the bar and restaurant business when he inherited a hotel from his father which was originally called the John J. Donohue Hotel. Later, the name was changed to the Black Sea Hotel in Garfield, New Jersey.

As my uncle John told me, "In the mid-1920s, a trainer for

the New York Yankees baseball team stumbled on the Black Sea. He told a member of the team, Babe Ruth, that he had found a 'hideaway' for him. A short drive from Yankee Stadium, the 'Babe' found the Black Sea to his liking, and he began to spend time there, partaking in adult refreshments and Jimmy's famous hot dogs, away from the crowds who incessantly hounded him for autographs.

"For a while, the Babe was able to enjoy the solitude of the Black Sea, but inevitably, word got around that Ruth was a patron. Ruth's big car, which bore New York license plates, was often seen outside. Fans started to flock, and Ruth took off.

"However, Jimmy and the Bambino had grown to be close friends, and Jimmy wasn't going to lose Ruth if he could help it. There was a garage across the street from the hotel, which Jimmy bought and had fixed up as private quarters for Ruth.

"When the Babe was able to drive right into the garage without being seen, he came back. Jimmy assigned a waiter to Ruth who would carry food and drinks over to the garage.

"The arrangement suited the Babe just fine, and he and Jimmy remained close friends and visited each other until just a few days before the Babe's death in 1948."

In September 2001, I visited the location in Garfield that, in the 1920s, had been the Black Sea Hotel and was now the Pescador restaurant. I asked for the owner, introduced myself, and asked her if I could see the room in the hotel reserved for Babe Ruth—before Jimmy had the garage next door built for him. The room was no more than 10' X 10', just large enough for a bed and perhaps a chair and a table on which Babe could be served Jimmy's famous hot dogs, beer, and who knows what else.

Sometime in the 1930s, Jimmy relocated his establishment from Garfield to Route 23 in Mountain View, New Jersey. What started as a roadside stand there became one of the most famous restaurants and nightclubs in the state. At one time the restaurant was serving up 1,300 meals at dinner hour, and patrons danced to some of the most famous big bands of the 1940s and '50s— Glen Miller, Tommy Dorsey, and Harry James.

The restaurant also featured a fast-food counter for motorists, and who was one of those in a white apron serving up the hot dogs to patrons? None other than Jimmy himself! Uncle Jim's "hands-on" approach, and his personal relationship with customers had a profound impact on me. It was a business model I tried to emulate during forty years of managing my own business.

My personal recollection of Jimmy was of his humility and generosity. My mother was Jimmy's niece, and during occasional outings in the 1940s to Mountain View for a "roadside" dinner of Jimmy's famous hot dogs, the food would not only be "on the house" but Jimmy would slip a $20 bill to each member of the family—at a time when my father was making no more than

$50/week! Jimmy knew where his niece had come from and how she must have been struggling to make ends meet. Jimmy's generosity was legendary.

I believe my relationship to Jimmy Donohue and the example he set for me was *divinely inspired*.

FLOYD CHESTER JOHNSON

IN 1946, IN a stroke of brilliance, my uncle Floyd came up with an idea for an ice cream parlor. The essential "ingredients" were all in place—a small existing building on Johnson property (formerly a florist shop owned by Anna and Fred and operated by Floyd) and six acres of property for a perfect-sized building and parking lot. I eavesdropped on the conversation on the night Floyd presented his idea to my father and showed him plans for the prospective building. On that night, the most productive phase of my father's life began (thirteen years of consecutive employment), and Floyd had proven himself to be the most intelligent, the most stable, the most skilled, and the hardest working of all six Johnson brothers.

Floyd's idea resulted in the production and distribution of

a high quality, delicious product for which there was a great demand, and dozens of high school students were given the opportunity to work in the store. If truth were known, Dean's mother Anna and father Fred were a major influence in my father, Dean, being involved in the partnership to open and run the business—a condition, I believe, for the use of their six acres of property.

The timing could not have been better. Throughout the 1930s and '40s, America was obsessed with all things ice cream. In New York alone, twenty million gallons of vanilla, chocolate, and strawberry ice cream were consumed in drug stores and soda fountains. A store devoted to just ice cream—from banana splits to egg creams to chocolate malts, all served up by "soda jerks" like me.

JAMES DONOHUE MURPHY

Jim Murphy & his wife Liz

DURING A TRIP to New Jersey in September 2000, on an impulse, I dropped into Cogans (formerly Allwood Rest)—a bar and grill on Bloomfield Avenue just a block south of where we lived on Scoles Avenue in the 1930s. The last I heard, the property was owned by my Grand Uncle Jimmy Donohue. I thought I'd stop in for a beer to see if I could learn anything about the whereabouts of Jimmy's grandson, Jim Murphy. After some casual small talk with the bartender, I asked him who the owner of this place was. What I learned from him would open for me an important contact and valuable information on the Donohue family history, with facts and photographs. He said, "He's a guy named Murphy who lives in Florida. When I signed the lease with him, he said I could stay as long as I wanted to, but he's sold the place out from under me. It will be demolished next week to make way for a medical building."

He was not too happy, but I could not have been more excited. I then asked him if he knew the name of the town Murphy lived in. I held my breath as he thumbed through some papers behind the bar. "Crystal Beach," he said. Bingo! "Thanks," I said. I put a generous tip on the bar and was on my way back to Virginia Beach.

The *divinely inspired* message in this story is that I had probably not been in this bar in nearly fifty years, but I showed up just hours before it was to be demolished! Had I not, I would never have learned of Jim Murphy's whereabouts, not known his friendship, nor shared with him many Donohue family stories.

PHYLLIS BRADY

IN NOVEMBER 1942, our family relocated again—a mere three blocks, from Scoles to Katherine Avenue. As a result of this move, more *divinely inspired* and life-altering events began to unfold.

Several houses up the street from us lived the Brady family— John, Phyllis, and son Jack. Born in April 1929, Jack Brady was three years older than me, but our proximity provided many opportunities for recreation and socializing—ping-pong in their basement, pitching a tennis ball against their front steps, basketball in the lot behind the Serwin house across the street.

While I was still in elementary school in the Allwood section of Clifton, Jack was already attending Pope Pius High School in Passaic where he lettered in three sports—baseball (third base), football (full-back), and basketball (guard). He was also president of his senior class!

Jack Brady was brilliant, but he was a paradox. At about five foot, six inches, he was a powerhouse on the athletic field, and I witnessed firsthand how brutal he could be in street fights. At the same time, he had the sensitivity of a fine artist. His pen, ink, and pencil sketches of Franklin Delano Roosevelt, General Douglas McArthur, General George Patton—and of me for which I sat for Jack for several hours while we sketched—were masterpieces!

Upon graduation from Pope Pius in 1946, Jack entered the Newark School of Fine and Industrial Art, from which he graduated in 1949. One of Jack's instructors at the school was Louis Kniep, Jr. Lou owned and operated an ad agency in Dover, New Jersey, with his wife Nancy. Lou must have recognized Jack's talent and work ethic at school, for he hired him immediately upon his graduation from NSFIA.

JACK & HIS MOTHER, PHYLLIS BRADY

Me at Sixteen Years Old and Jack Brady

JACK BRADY WAS a talent, but he was all about Jack. He was not one to think about others or share. He suffered, I believe, from "only-child syndrome." However, his mother, Phyllis, was just the opposite; she devoted her life to others. She was a teacher at St. Nicholas Catholic School in Passaic and treated me as one of her children. She was responsible, I believe, for the many times I was invited to join the Brady family on vacations in Cape Cod. I believe Mrs. Brady saw me as Jack's younger brother, and she was a big influence in events that were to follow in my life.

I had some idea of what I wanted to do after high school—

perhaps something to do with pencil and pen-and-ink sketches and oil paintings; I enjoyed the recognition it occasionally brought. Fortunately for me, it turned out to be an interest which would lead to a marketable skill.

My plan, upon graduation from high school in 1950, was to follow Jack's example and enroll in NSFIA. But Jack needed an assistant/intern at the agency at which he had been hired, so Jack and Lou Kniep called me to a meeting at the agency in December 1950 and offered me an opportunity I could not refuse. It didn't take much to persuade me to come to work at the agency and go to NSFIA evening school. By agreeing to their proposal, my life was set on a path that would guide me for the next seventy years—a path, by the way, which was established not by me but by others. Jack Brady? Most likely by Mrs. Phyllis Brady, who would be looking out not only for her son but for me for whom I believe she had great affection! Soon after that meeting, with the promise of a job and with the help of a down payment from my mother, I bought a near-new 1949 Chevrolet coupe for the commute to work. In December 1950, I began employment at Kniep Ad Agency at $25/week and attending NSFIA evening school.

I believe that every piece in my career puzzle, guided by *divine inspiration*, was fitting together perfectly—live at home with my parents, go to school at night, learn things I needed to know on the job, perform a job with which I felt comfortable and with which I was well suited, make enough to put gas in my car, and make car payments, and still have some time to spare. At $25/week, the job wasn't one I took for the money; I loved what I was learning in school at night and loved what I was doing on the job.

Jack Brady was a super talent—in academics (president of his high school senior class), in athletics (he was offered a position on a minor league baseball team), and in creative art—a borderline genius in my opinion. I was blessed by my mother's decision to relocate from Scoles Avenue just three blocks north to Katherine Avenue and just a few houses from the Brady's.

Jack was the only kid on the block who was close to me in age. His mother Phyllis was a teacher at St. Nichols Parochial School in Passaic. She knew I came from good families in the neighborhood on both the Donohue and Johnson sides, and she encouraged the friendship between me and Jack. I would see her getting off the Passaic-Allwood-Bloomfield bus on her way home from work. She was responsible, I'm sure, for my being invited to Cape Cod on summer vacations almost as a member of the family, and to New York, along the Hudson River, to picnic and swim. We practically became part of the Brady family. Phyllis and my mother became very close friends.

1949 Rendering by Jack

LOUIS KNIEP, JR.

Lou, Jack Brady, and Nancy Kniep, 1950s

MY FIRST TERM of employment at Kniep Associates was 1950-1953; my second term, after military service, was 1956-1961. Other than my father at Johnson's Ice Cream Bar, Lou Kniep was my first real employer; and like a father, Lou took me under his wing. Lou was extremely talented—not only in graphics and package design, but in building construction, interior design, landscaping, plumbing, and mechanical and electrical work.

Starting in 1946, Lou and his wife Nancy did an amazing job of re-building a 117-year-old grist mill in Dover, New Jersey, into a beautiful home. Building an art studio next to the mill and building a summer home on Meddybemps Island in Maine—you name it, Lou could do it. Where the water wheel once turned in the mill, Lou converted the space into a studio where, in 1946, he "hung out his shingle" as an Industrial Designer. In 1949, Lou started to take on advertising work. This was the year in which he hired Jack Brady as art director. It was on September 6, 1950, that Lou filed for the trade name: Louis Kniep, Jr. and Associates.

Short-term, this was a win-win for both Jack and Lou. Jack was also very talented and hard-working. Having Jack in the studio to handle design and production assignments left Lou free to solicit new business and service accounts. Lou's formula seemed to be working. At the time, the Redbook of Advertising Agencies listed twenty-six accounts for Kniep Associates Country Ad Agency.

Kniep Associates was known as an "industrial ad agency," meaning he specialized in graphic design, advertising, and marketing for industrial manufacturers, as opposed to consumer product companies. Today those agencies are known as "business-to-business."

Sixty-five years after I started at Kniep Associates, I was still in the business of "business-to-business" advertising—a testament to Lou's genius in narrowing his target market to one that would endure.

Most of the 1950s were a peaceful time for Lou and his family. But that was destined to change. No one could ever have imagined the tragedies that were to overtake Lou and Nancy Kniep starting in the late 1950s.

Kniep Compound in 1969. Aerial Photo taken by me

US ARMY SERVICE

IN AN IMPULSIVE move, a few days after my twenty-first birthday in 1953, I drove to California with a friend from Passaic and held a job for a few months as a carpenter's helper. The work was hard, and the southern California heat was oppressive, but my options were limited.

On July 7, 1953, I was stunned to receive a draft notice in the mail to report immediately to Ft. Ord, California. Without hesitation, I called my draft board in Paterson and persuaded them to allow me to be drafted from there instead of from California. "If you can be here a week from today, we can make it happen," they said. That was incredibly fortunate. They could just as easily have said, "You left us and went to California; now it's your problem."

I reported on time and began military service on July 10, 1953, just seventeen days before the end of the Korean conflict. A brief period of processing was followed by sixteen weeks of grueling basic infantry training in Ft. Dix, New Jersey.

I found army basic training challenging and even considered applying to Officer Candidate School, but ultimately decided to try to find ways and places I could be of value to my country other than being an infantryman or a leader of infantrymen in the army.

I requested a meeting with the recruiting sergeant to discuss army school options, which would be offered to me if I agreed to serve an additional three years in the regular army. The recruiting sergeant handed me a stapled booklet of mimeographed sheets with a listing of all the schools offered by the army—cook school, maintenance mechanic school, crane operator school, truck driver school; in the seemingly endless list, nothing seemed appropriate for me. At the suggestion of the sergeant, I started again from page one. On my second time through the list— BINGO!—photo school jumped off the page!

On November 3, 1953, I was discharged from the US Army and became a "Regular Army" private. This moment was, like so many other events in my journey, I believe, *divinely inspired*.

Following sixteen weeks of Infantry Basic Training were twelve weeks of intense, extremely informative, educational, professional photographic training in Ft. Monmouth, New Jersey.

I was then faced with the uncertainty of what was to be the most important turning point in my life until now—one over which I had absolutely no control. I remember trembling a bit as I stood in line waiting to read the bulletin board, which listed the *zone* to which each member of my leadership class was being assigned. The question that gave me pause was: would my gamble to give the army an additional thirty-six months of service in exchange for photo school pay off? Or would I wind up a rifleman in Korea after all? Call it the grace of God or *divine inspiration*, but I was the only member of my leadership class to be assigned to Germany! The rest of the class was sent to Korea where, fortunately for them, the conflict was winding down.

To whomever made that decision somewhere in the bowels of the army bureaucracy, I owe a lifelong debt of gratitude.

Again, with the greatest of good fortune, I was assigned to a photo lab in a quaint, beautiful town in Germany called Bad Kreuznach.

From the time I arrived in Bad K in May 1954 until February 1955, I worked in the photo lab at Signal Corp headquarters, during which I gained more valuable photographic experience for what was to follow—not only in my next army assignment but during my entire post-army career!

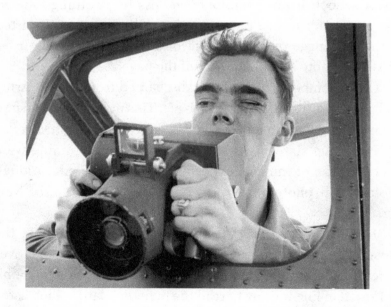

Operating 4x5 Aerial Reconnaissance Camera

BOB PARKER & MR. HARRELL

Bob Parker in Garmisch-Partenkirchen

IN DECEMBER 1954, at the suggestion of a fellow in the photo lab named Bob Parker, we took a three-day leave and applied for "temporary duty" with the Army ski patrol in Garmisch Partenkirchen, Germany. The mission of the ski patrol was to oversee the safety of those in the military.

When Parker and I returned to Bad Kreuznach, Mr. Harrell, the warrant officer in charge of the photo lab said to me, "I won't refuse your request for ski patrol, but if you'll forego it, I'll offer you the option of a one-month 'test' TDY [temporary duty] in either Mainz, Mannheim, or Baumholder to be the field photographer there."

However, Mr. Harrell strongly recommended Baumholder be my choice because, he said, "it will offer you many opportunities to practice photography." You'll be housed in a bachelor officer's apartment, have your own 4x5 speed graphic, your own custom photo lab, as many supplies of film and flash bulbs as you need, and a reporter will be assigned to work with you, and you'll have your own jeep. Assignments will come once a week from headquarters' public relations office."

There was no way I could refuse Mr. Harrell's offer. The calculated risk paid off! The result was photo lab and photographic experience with over 250 photos published in *Stars and Stripes*, in the division newspaper, *Hell on Wheels*, and other publications. Some were sent over the wire services—AP and UP—and some even published in the *Saturday Evening Post*!

How good, how fortunate, how *divinely inspired* was this for me? It was practically an extension of some of what I had been doing at Kniep's and preparation for what I hoped to do when I returned!

After I accepted Mr. Harrell's offer, the "test" one-month TDY extended to twenty-one months. My lifestyle and future were again to be dramatically impacted in a positive way.

The one-month TDY, which started in January 1955, was extended one month at a time until my rotation back to the states and discharge from the Army in October 1956. This "TDY" provided me with valuable experiences—experiences I could hardly have gained in any other way, having a lifelong impact on both my personal and professional lives. Never in my wildest dreams did I think that military service could offer the long-term benefits that it did!

The value of the photographic training I received in the army—not only during photo school in Ft. Monmouth but in my first assignment to the photo lab in Bad Kreuznach, and in the twenty-one-month temporary duty assignment in Baumholder—was, in my mind, *divinely inspired.*

At every stage of my seventy-year professional career, my experience with a camera and my graphic arts background paid dividends. The opportunities my camera gave me, especially in the army, seemed, at times, miraculous.

My twenty-one-month TDY in Baumholder was so achievement-oriented, so productive, that it went by so quickly; it was like a miniature version of our life on earth, *a wisp of smoke.*

LORI EBER

LORI EBER, A civilian living in Bad Kreuznach, somehow gained permission for easy access to the army compound called Foch Kaserne. I met him in the recreation hall where a group would meet for relaxation and occasional ping-pong. I played him a few times. He called me his "Master."

Over time, Lori and I struck up a friendship. He took me for rides around the local Bad Kreuznach area on his motorcycle, took me to his home for dinner with his family, and invited me to his sister Evelyn's wedding.

Lori was also the son of the owner of an MG Automobile dealership in Bad Kreuznach, Edgar Eber. One day in 1955, Lori mentioned to me casually that his father's dealership had purchased a near-new MG TF 1500. The original owner was an Air Force pilot who had unexpectedly been reassigned to the US. I asked Lori what his father was asking for the car. Lori said he would ask him and let me know.

The next day, Lori said, "My father will sell it to you for what he paid for it: $1,100." (MSRP was $1,995.) We went immediately to the dealership to look at it. It was in pristine condition; the odometer read less than 5,000 miles.

I had already calculated that I could swing it. My army salary as a PFC was $105/month. With food and clothing supplied by the army, my expenses were almost zero. I had an allotment of two cartons of cigarettes/week at $1.00/carton. I didn't smoke; when adding the profits from the sale of the cigarettes I sold, I was left with more than $135/month—more than enough to make the payments on the car.

My meeting and friendship with Lori Eber, which I believe to be *divinely inspired*, provided me with a unique lifestyle and life-altering opportunities during the balance of my service in the army!

The US Army shipped my car home for $1.

PHIL VANCE & MANOOCH

With Manooch in 1952

FRIENDSHIPS WERE NOT something I made easily—not in elementary school, nor in high school. Cousin Ken Stewart and neighbor Jack Brady were somewhat "friends," but Ken was part of the family, and Jack was three years older than me.

While in high school, I had but one date—with a neighbor named Dorothy Reynics. I never asked her; she asked me. I hardly knew her. She must have been desperate for a date to her school prom to ask me.

Following high school, I was part of a crowd that moved from Herm and Lou's luncheonette on Broadway in Passaic to Leo's Bar and Grill across the street. Most of the "crowd" I was in were lovable, Passaic "dese, dems, and dose" guys.

Carmine (Manooch) Cresenta was my closest friend. We started kindergarten on the same day. It was at Leo's Bar and

Grill that Carmine said to me one night, *"Bobby, you have to get out of this gang. You can do more with your life. You can say those big words."*

At that moment, my life changed forever. Thanks to Carmine, I thought about myself differently. I never forgot his words. These were words of wisdom coming from a friend who had less than a high school education and whose father, it was rumored, was a member of the Mafia.

I left for California shortly after, then I was drafted. I never returned to the "gang." I never saw "Manooch" again.

Phil Vance, whom I met in the Public Information Office in Bad Kreuznach in 1954, enjoyed many of the privileges I didn't—relatively well-to-do parents and a good education. But somehow, Phil and I bonded and formed a friendship which would last for more than sixty-five years. Phil, who was born in Springfield, Illinois, but did post-graduate work on a Fulbright Scholarship at the University of Oslo, was non-standard. He had everyone in the Public Information Office convinced, including me, that he was Norwegian. He pretended not to understand any instruction he was given with which he did not agree.

Meeting and having Phil as a friend, combined with my army experiences in Germany, was a great education in itself.

In February 1956, I drove from Baumholder, Germany, to Oslo, Norway, for a skiing vacation with Phil. On the way to Oslo, somewhere in Sweden, a tire on the MG blew out on a sub-zero, windswept, lonely road, which was beginning to darken. The wheel spinner, which secures the wheel to the axel, was frozen to the axle! I honestly believed I would freeze to death on this deserted road trying to remove it—one of several near-death experiences I experienced in my life. Somehow, I managed to hammer the spinner off moments before my hands (and perhaps I) would have frozen. By the grace of God, I somehow made it to the next town where I found a service station to repair the tire.

Squint 1955

Squint 1997

Phil in 1955 and 1997.
At home among his friends, he was referred to as "Squint."
After sixty-six years, our friendship continues.

THE HOSPITALITY OF STRANGERS IN SPAIN

Trousers got soaked helping a crew bring a capsized sailboat ashore following a sudden gale along the Italian Riviera. August 19, 1956.

DURING MY THIRTY-MONTH military tour in Europe, I had done some traveling, but I decided that one grand tour of areas I had not yet seen would be time well spent. After spending a day in Rüdesheim with Marga Fechter, the beautiful sister of a fellow with whom I played some ping-pong in Baumholder, I left Bad Kreuznach and headed to Paris on August 9, 1956.

During the trip, I had an extremely stressful "good news, bad news" experience and a meeting that would change my life forever.

Until August 13, the trip was, for the most part, uneventful. I made Paris in one day and hated it. Traffic was a perpetual gridlock, and because of my nonexistent French language skills, it was nearly impossible for me to find anything. It was dark when I arrived; I couldn't ride around all night, so I found a hotel that cost almost as much as I had budgeted for the entire day! I couldn't wait to get out of Paris.

The next morning—August 11—I enjoyed one of the finest and cheapest breakfasts I'd had in any restaurant anywhere—at the American Embassy! Of course, I did manage to make a few stops that day—the typical tourist destinations—at the Eiffel Tower, the Louvre, the Champs Elysées, and Pigalle. That night, I returned to the embassy for a pork dinner and bought three sandwiches and a jug of red wine for the trip the next day.

After a stop in Bordeaux on the 13th, I had one of the most eventful (and stressful) days of the trip. It started at 6:00 A.M. with a short five-mile drive outside of town to an air force base for breakfast.

Destination: Madrid. My first shock was at customs where they charged a $1.25 toll for which I hadn't budgeted.

The drive over the mountains was very difficult; the road was bumpy, winding, and steep. The rest of the road to "here" was not bad. The bad news was, however, that I could not say where "here" was because I had no idea where I was (other than in a small village) when the MG's engine quit.

It was extremely hot that day. *The gas line may have a vapor lock*, I thought. I let the engine cool and tried again to start it, without success.

Onlookers started to gather; they were fascinated by the car. They had probably never seen an MG. I tried asking the locals standing around for the location of a bank where I could cash a traveler's check. They made it clear to me that the bank was closed. One fellow offered me the equivalent of $15.50 until it opened. There was not a car in sight in this town, so I doubted if anyone would know how to fix an MG. I didn't think things could get worse, but they did! I tried again to start the engine and it would not even turn over!

With the help of some of the villagers gathered around the car, we pushed it to the garage of a nearby hotel. The owner of the hotel asked me if I wanted a mechanic to look at the engine. I got across to him that I would like to wait until *"mañana,"* but I didn't know how to explain to him that I wanted to wait until I had some money to pay for repairs. He ignored me and called a mechanic. A mechanic soon arrived. It took him all of fifteen minutes and $.25 in labor to fix whatever the problem was.

By this time, it was too late to continue to Madrid, so I asked for a room in the hotel for the night and got ready for dinner, both of which made me very uneasy. The room they offered smelled musty—the mattress was damp—like it hadn't been slept in or cleaned in years; the room had no running water, and the door could be closed but not locked.

As I passed by the restaurant in which dinner was to be served, I was shocked to see it swarming with flies! I'd never seen anything like it. But to me, staying here was better than taking a chance on breaking down somewhere in the middle of the night between here and Madrid.

While waiting for dinner—which was to be served at 11:00 P.M.—the two *mecanicos* that had worked on the car, and two other men from the village, signaled to me to come with them. I had no choice but to go along with whatever it was they had in mind.

They headed out of town, down a very narrow and lonely road. It was starting to get dark, and I was starting to feel very uneasy. After about a thirty-minute walk, we approached the side of a hill in which there was an entrance to what looked like a cave. I followed the group into the cave, which was not only pitch-dark but cold and damp.

I had no idea where I was, or what the folks I was following had in mind for me. I felt more vulnerable than I ever had in my life. I could die here, and no one would ever know what happened to me.

As we walked deeper into the cave, it got a bit brighter from a lantern. I could make out to the left what looked like a long, wooden drinking trough for animals. A frail-looking elderly woman seemed to appear out of nowhere, carrying a large jug on her shoulder. She poured some wine out of the jug, which apparently had been filled from kegs stored further back in the cave, into the trough. It didn't seem to bother her or anyone else that there were a countless number of flies in the trough, many of which were dead and floating in the wine.

From the trough, the wine was then ladled into a large glass that had a narrow neck and a funnel-like spout. When the glass was tilted, the wine poured out of the spout and into one's mouth without the glass touching any lips. This vessel was passed around to everyone sitting around the trough, from which we all drank.

After nearly two hours of drinking this "cave wine," on the way back to the hotel, I felt very relieved that my drinking friends had nothing in mind for me other than drinking and, at that point, I was too inebriated to care.

Back at the hotel, we all enjoyed dinner, which included an omelet, wine, boiled potatoes and gravy, more wine, pork chops, and more wine. At the hotel were two touring Englishmen. Together we had another six rounds of martinis at $.20/round. Prior to leaving in the morning, I made my best efforts to pay for the hospitality of these wonderful people of this village, but to no avail.

They would take not one *paseta* for the hotel room, the meals, or the wine. For the car repair, they took twenty-five cents for the two *mechanicos*. They did succeed, however, in making me feel guilty for thinking they had anything other than my well-being and their generous hospitality in mind. My two regrets were (1) that I did not take a group picture of me with the wonderful people of this small village and (2) that I did not make a note in my diary of the name of this beautiful village.

My next destination, Madrid, was notable again for hospitality. I was already way over budget. I had just $60 in American Express checks and 880 *pasetas* (about $22) with seventeen days left on the trip.

The folks with whom I stayed at the Residencia Arizona were more than generous; for three days, my stay, the room, and meals were just $3.75, which included washing and pressing my clothes.

The next day, August 18, I was up at 6:30, had breakfast, rotated the tires, and headed for Barcelona. Again, the ride was not easy. It was only 188 miles, but it took nearly six hours. The roads were climbing, twisting, and generally rough. The hotel I found in Barcelona—the Victoria—was $4 a day with meals.

Next destination: Nice, France!

The trip to Nice was 560 miles and fifteen hours, but it wasn't bad. Good music all the way and some beautiful views going over the Massif des Maures mountain range between Marseille and Nice.

I almost ran off the road, however, at the first sight of a young lady in a bikini. I had never seen anything like it in public.

That night, I stayed in a camping *platz* ten kilometers outside of Nice to make up for the extravagances in Barcelona.

JAN CARLSSON

Jan was not only a scholarship track star at the University of Michigan but, as you can see from this photo taken the day after we met in Nice, he was a skilled diver.

JAN CARLSSON, AN itinerant traveler from Sweden, was a student on a track scholarship at the University of Michigan in Ann Arbor. He was hitchhiking around Europe with a friend and fellow student named Dick Hill.

On this day, a man on a scooter stopped and offered one of them a ride into Nice, France. Jan and Dick flipped a coin to determine who would join him on the ride. The coin fell in Jan's favor. This coin flip on a street on the outskirts of Nice, France, would impact my future for the rest of my life.

Jan's scooter driver dropped him off near a USO (United Service Organization) in Nice. Jan walked into the USO just moments before I did. We were both going in for the same reason—free doughnuts and coffee.

While waiting in line for our coffee, Jan and I struck up a conversation, ate, then played some ping-pong in the recreation area of the USO. His English was so good, I thought he was American. I invited Jan to do some sightseeing with me. We started by visiting the beaches in Nice, then Jan joined me on my trip. The next day, we drove to the beach at Cannes, which, pleasantly, was mostly sand, not rocks. We found a hotel in Cannes for $1 each.

I found in Jan a good source for money-saving ideas—finding cheap places to stay, to eat, having cookies and coffee at the USO, and at times, skipping meals.

One of our first stops was to try water skiing at Juan le Pin. Since this was my first attempt at water skiing, the serviceman in charge offered a brief lesson for beginners. He explained the process of sitting on the dock holding onto a bar (fastened to the cable connected to the boat) until the boat moved forward and the cable became taut, at which time I was to let myself be pulled off the dock, allowing the skis to hit the surface of the water with the tips up.

For some reason, I slipped off the dock prior to the line being taut and found myself standing with my skis in mud in about ten feet of water. I was then faced with the challenge of patiently holding my breath and waiting for the line to become taut. When it did, I faced yet another problem—maintaining my grip on the bar against the tremendous force of the water being pushed against my chest as the boat sped forward. Barely able to hold on or keep the ski tips up, I finally surfaced to see the two servicemen who were piloting the boat laughing hysterically. On August 24, Jan and I had planned to go to the pool in Monte

Carlo for a change, but entry to the pool was 500 francs, so we went to the free beach, changed, and swam the quarter mile to the beach that adjoined the pool. I was forced to swim with one hand as I held my camera in the other.

We had a glorious day there, rubbing elbows with the elite, diving, and sunning. On the way back, we used the free bus service that the Metropole Hotel had for its guests.

After somewhat uneventful stops in Genoa, Milano, Verona, Lake Garda, Venice, Innsbruck, Schaffenhausen, St. Anton, Liechtenstein, and Zurich, I dropped Jan off in Germany, and he continued to hitch-hike his way back to Sweden. I continued on my trip and arrived back in Baumholder on August 31.

But, fortunately, this was not the last I would see of Jan Carlsson.

Jan Carlsson, my dear friend of 66 years,
passed away on May 27, 2022.

JAN CARLSSON &
GRANT SCRUGGS

IN DECEMBER 1956, Jan Carlsson visited the US and stayed at my parents' home in Clifton. He was on his way to Jamestown, New York, to take a teaching position. During his stay, I accompanied Jan to New York to visit a teammate of his on the track team at Michigan named Grant Scruggs. Grant was a quarter-miler and still active in track as a member of the New York Athletic Club.

Once Jan was on his way to Jamestown, Grant and I stayed in touch. I often accompanied him to training sessions at the Club and drove him to meets in the Metropolitan area. The NYAC was also a social center for us, and we played an occasional game of ping-pong between his training sessions.

I have a scale to which I measure people's character, an SOS scale, symbols over substance. As I was to learn, Grant Scruggs was considerably more symbolic than substantial, except when it came to running. He could run like a deer.

Jan's visit to Clifton was followed by my trip in August 1958 to Jan's parent's farm, Björka, in Locknevi, Sweden. The first thing I learned when I arrived at Jan's house was that he was not the poor itinerant traveler I thought he was. His home, by Sweden standards, was a mansion. His parent's farm was large enough to be found on maps of Sweden. His family was in the very profitable business of selling logs to pulp mills. The family house was on a lake used for swimming and boating, surrounded by small homes which they rented out to vacationers.

On my return from Sweden, expecting my father to pick me up at Newark Airport, I was shocked to find Grant waiting for me in my car with an aspiring opera singer I was seeing named Mary Nettum. I realized that Grant Scruggs was not only a fast runner but a fast talker. He had telephoned my mother in New York, talked her out of the keys to my car, somehow made his way to 37 Katherine Avenue in Clifton, collected my car keys from my mother, then used my car as a moving van to move the contents of Mary's apartment (where she was living with Grant on 89th Street) to an apartment on the Lower East Side which she had rented while I was in Sweden. Grant had no license to drive a car. I was shocked that he even knew how to drive a car, never mind a stick-shift Beetle. My mother was a softy and a people-pleaser. Grant was too strong and talked too fast for her.

I was outraged! But I didn't make a fuss about it; I didn't want my mother to be caught in a dispute between me and Grant. But I believe it turned out to be a blessing. I learned who Grant Scruggs really was.

My relationships with both Grant and Mary were never the same. I stopped seeing Mary in early 1959. Mary and Grant were married sometime thereafter.

Grant and I crossed paths during the early 1990s when he made a surprise visit to our home in Kinnelon. The reason for his visit remains a mystery to me. I have no idea what the visit was about—why he made his way all the way from Manhattan to Kinnelon other than that Grant told me that he was in contact with my friend, Marty Reisman.

The next time I spoke to Marty, I asked him what he had heard about Grant. He told me that Grant and Mary had a falling out because Grant insisted on a share of the money she had inherited from her parents, and she refused. My suspicions about him—that he was a fast-talking snake-oil salesman—were confirmed. Grant Scruggs taught me a lesson about human behavior that I never knew before but have since never forgotten.

BERNIE BUKIET I

IN APRIL 1957, while browsing in a Manhattan Barnes & Noble, I stumbled across Coleman Clark's little sports library book, *Table Tennis*, published in 1948. I thumbed through it and came across a chapter, "Thumbnail Sketches of the World's Best." There, I read with great interest profiles of players like Sol Schiff, Dick Miles, Lou Pagliaro, and Marty Reisman, all of whom were New Yorkers. Table tennis had held a fascination for me since I played Jack Brady in his basement in the early 1940s. Jack was three years older than me and extremely athletic and competitive. He could beat me sitting in a chair and spotting me fifteen points in a twenty-one-point game. I played some on a concrete table in Third Ward Park and played some in the army in the 1950s. I thought to myself, *How good can these guys be??*

Needless to say, I bought the book for $1.25. At my first opportunity, I was on a mission to seek out where these world class players played—eager to see what world-class table tennis looked like.

The next day, I returned to the city. I recalled seeing a red neon table tennis sign in a window on the second floor of a building near Times Square. I went upstairs to a large room of tables but no players. One of the men just hanging out asked me if I wanted to play. I told him I wasn't interested but that I was looking for the place where players by the name of Miles, Schiff, Pagliaro, and Reisman played.

"They play uptown," he said. "You wanna go there?"

He introduced himself. His name was Paul Moorat. He gave me directions.

I got back in the car and headed from Times Square up Broadway to 96th Street. Above the door to the basement of a building on the northwest corner of 96th and Broadway was a small sign—*Riverside Table Tennis*. I walked down the few steps to the darkened basement. Sitting behind a desk just inside the doorway smoking a cigarette was a man in his mid-thirties.

He said to me in a strong Eastern European accent, "You play ping-pong?"

"No," I said. "I don't know how to play." I had a feeling his question would involve money, and I had just enough for the next few days to cover gas and tolls. "I Bernie Bukiet. I US champion," he said. "You have big country here. How come you can't find someone beat me?"

Bernie was the first real table tennis player I had ever met. He had just returned from South Bend, Indiana, where he had won the US Men's Singles Championship. Bernie had done more in his brief career than just win the US Men's. In 1953, he defeated four-time National Champion Lou Pagliaro to win the Canadian National Exhibition (CNE) Open.

In 1954, at thirty-five, Bernie had been picked as a member of the '54 US Team to the London World's. At the Wembley venue, he reached the high point of his career. He got to the quarters of the Men's Singles before losing to the winner, Ichiro Ogimura—a result that'd give Bernie, playing with a hard rubber racket to Ichiro's foam bat, a #5 World Ranking.

LOUIS KNIEP, JR.

**Lou with our two-year old son, Eric, in July 1968.
Lou was such a good soul.**

AWARE OF MY growing interest in table tennis, Lou set up a ping-pong table in the room in his home set aside for entertaining and recreation. Lou's thoughtfulness provided an opportunity for practice during lunch hours with a new practice partner— Jack Brady!

By 1958, the tables had turned. Jack could no longer dominate me, let alone beat me playing in a chair as he had in the Brady basement in the 1940s. Between lessons with Mr. Lawrence and playing time in New York, my game was evolving rapidly. But as athletic and competitive as he was, Jack also picked up on proper techniques quickly. He soon became a worthy practice partner for me.

The table tennis skills that Jack was developing in Lou's rec room would soon pay off for him big time in the business world and would have a *divinely inspired*, long-term, positive impact on me and my family forever!

Meanwhile, the lifestyle Lou had created for himself, Nancy, and their employees had become too casual to last. As Lou told a Newark *Star-Ledger* reporter, "We have coffee breaks, and when the weather gets warm, we have swimming breaks. When a designing problem gets tough or a slogan just won't come, an employee can just let his imagination soar while he takes a dip or casts a fishing fly in the brook behind the house." SOS, Lou!

One day, Lou had it with the idealistic "country ad agency" atmosphere he had created. "We've got to start getting more work done around here," he declared. "We're not running a country club. We're running an ad agency," he said. Cracks were starting to appear in Lou's system!

One seemingly ordinary morning in 1959, while preparing my schedule for the day, I received an ominous intercom call from Lou Kniep. Lou wasted no time in asking, "Where's Jack?"

"I don't know, Lou. It was his turn to drive, and he called last night and said he wasn't coming in today," I said.

"Come down to my office immediately," he said. When I got to his office, Lou was visibly shaken. "I can't reach any of our customers," he said. "Not Jerry Monahan [one of Lou's best friends and best accounts, A.P. Smith], not McKiernan-Terry [his best account], not Taylor-Wharton [his oldest account]. I'll keep trying, but this does not look good, Dean," he said. (Turning the business over to Jack . . . bad move, Lou.) "Will you help me rebuild?" he asked. I told him in no uncertain terms and without hesitation that I would stay and do what I could to help him rebuild the business.

Lou and I immediately began to research target accounts to call on in northern New Jersey and to plan for each of us to branch out and start soliciting target companies. Glynn Roberts also stayed on and did a wonderful job of servicing the art needs of accounts that Lou and I were able to bring in.

Unfortunately, this was just the first in a series of events that would befall Lou and Nancy Kniep—one of which resulted in a tragic loss of two lives.

Leaping forward, Helga and I did not see nor hear much of Nancy and Lou Kniep. When I did talk to Lou, he was always up-beat, but below the surface, as I heard from Glynn Roberts, things were not going well. Lou was being treated for cancer, and his family life was dysfunctional; he was estranged from both of his boys (Kip and Jerry) who had relocated to Tennessee and who were not on speaking terms with each other. Lou and Nancy's lives were seriously out of balance.

On December 30, 1985, two friends of Lou and Nancy's, Paul and Mary Underwood, were paying a visit for the holidays. That night, Paul was the last to retire. About 2:00 A.M., Lou was awakened by a smoke alarm. He found the house in ablaze. He went down to the kitchen to try to extinguish the flames, but they were already too intense, and he could not get back up the stairs. He tried to climb a ladder from the outside to get into the second-floor bedrooms through a window, but he could not because of the heat and smoke. The fire department had determined that Paul Underwood had apparently thrown a cigarette butt, which had not been extinguished, into the kitchen trash.

What was thought to be the bodies of Mary and Paul Underwood were later found—dead from smoke inhalation and fire. The person thought to be Nancy Kniep was found alive but severely burned. The house was all but gutted.

However, that was not the end of this terrible tragedy. Three days after the fire, the Morris County Medical Examiner reported a case of mistaken identity. The female victim in the fire, thought to be Mary Underwood, was Nancy Kniep! The error was discovered when Mary Underwood, heavily bandaged and sedated, regained consciousness, and the nurse caring for her addressed her as "Nancy."

"I'm not Nancy," she said, "I'm Mary."

Lou, of course, went into shock when he heard the news. By this time, Nancy's body had been cremated on instructions from the Underwood family. The day after this awful news, the studio, which was attached to the house by a breezeway, was set ablaze by a space heater which Lou was using to keep warm. Most of the building was also gutted along with all of his customer artwork and files! This was followed by a fire which gutted his summer home in Maine.

What on earth did this wonderful man do to suffer these horrible events? How could Lou survive the emotional devastation of these multiple tragedies? Through action, achievement, and perseverance! He spent the next three years rebuilding the house, the studio, and the house in Maine.

My friend and mentor Louis Kniep, Jr. died of cancer on February 1, 1990, at the age of seventy-six.

With a view of the rear-view mirror, I can see more clearly how Lou Kniep's career evolved.

He started as a gifted talent, as an artist and designer. Lou could do everything—graphic design, all things building, electrical, and mechanical. His multiple talents guided him to a level of success which, unfortunately, led him into a series of traps and dangerous pitfalls—overconfidence (boastfully claiming often, "I have built a million-dollar ad agency," which was never the case), placing symbols over substance (boats, sports cars, and his house in Meddybemps), and having "friends" that had a level of "celebrity" (Paul and Mary Underwood).

I met Paul Underwood several times and found him to have an elitist attitude over the fact that he had a high position at *The New York Times*. The loss of work ethic led Lou to focus on leisure pursuits, which allowed others (Jack Brady) to move into the vacuum created by Lou—the hard work necessary to keep the agency successful (design, customer service, and follow-up) falling by the wayside.

Lou saw himself as leading an elitist lifestyle, but in reality, in my opinion, he was falling into a series of pitfalls that led to issues of life and death.

I have a lot for which to be grateful to Lou Kniep. He brought me into his agency when I had nothing to offer but a high school diploma and a willingness to work hard for very little. He made me feel a part of his family; he treated me like a son. He was a very good and kind man. I don't believe he deserved what happened to him, starting with Jack Brady stealing his business. But who am I to say?

Lou in 1959; the year that Jack Brady revealed who he really was.

ROGERS CASE

JUST ABOUT THE time my list of potential clients in north Jersey was becoming exhausted—and what work there was to be done in the art department was being handled by Glynn Roberts—out of the blue, in what I believe was clearly a *divinely inspired* event, I was offered a marketing position in a company owned by a fellow named Rogers Case, a table tennis player whom I met at the Cranford, New Jersey, club.

I left Kniep's for the last time and joined Rogers' in August 1961.

Rogers Case was extremely wealthy—a multimillionaire when having a million meant something. Rogers was born into an elite, high-class family. He inherited a company called Transandean Associates from his father, Daniel Rogers Case. The company not only owned the telephone system in Colombia, South America, but it manufactured and marketed telephone line accessories which were designed and patented by his father. Not only was his father considered a genius in the way he carved a telephone system out of the jungles of Colombia, but his grandfather was a famous American Navy Rear, Admiral Augustus Ludlow Case.

Transandean Associates was run by a man named Raul Gutierrez who had worked for Daniel Rogers Case in Colombia. He knew the business thoroughly—from the Colombian side to the American side. He handled bookkeeping and shipment of the transposition brackets and insulators from a warehouse which was a short walk from the office on Main Street in Orange, New Jersey. (Raul and I were working in this warehouse on the day president John Kennedy was assassinated.) Raul referred to Mr. Case as "the genius who built an empire from bed." (Mr. Case was disabled in his later years, Raul told me, from later stages of diabetes which required amputation of his legs.)

I never met Rogers' father but, according to Raul, he was a brilliant entrepreneur who not only built the telephone system in Colombia, South America, but built a financial empire based on his invention of the transposition bracket. Working with a man named Dr. Ferrero (who was in his nineties when I met him in December 1962 and who worked with Guglielmo Marconi in the development of the telephone and his pioneering work on long-distance radio transmission), Mr. Case assembled a team of technicians and laborers who placed the poles and strung the lines through the jungles and over the Andes Mountains to bring telephone communications to the country. In building the telephone system in Colombia, Mr. Case developed and patented the "transposition bracket" which transposed telephone lines on both the telephone pole and mid-span lines—a necessary procedure to eliminate "cross-talk" between wires. He used the product extensively in Columbia and also marketed it to telephone companies in the US, mainly Western Electric. When Rogers' father died in April 1954, Rodgers was given a hardship discharge from the US Army, and he inherited control of Transandean Associates.

Rogers' mother Ethel and sister Muriel showed up at the office occasionally but were not involved in running the business in any meaningful way. Rogers' staff in Bogota, Colombia, in 1963 numbered about fifteen, including Dr. Ferrero.

When I joined the company and learned of the revenue stream coming in from Colombia (in management fees) and

Western Electric (in profits), I was stunned by the numbers.

The friendship with Rogers suited me perfectly. The business was highly profitable, so the atmosphere and the work schedule at his office in Orange, New Jersey, was casual. Rogers paid me nearly twice what I was making at Kniep's, which helped further subsidize my table tennis.

The increase in pay also allowed me to move out of my parents' home and into an apartment in the new, luxury Country Club Towers in Clifton, New Jersey. It marked the beginning of a new and very different lifestyle for me. At twenty-nine, I was finally leaving home for the last time. The timing of this move, in September 1961, out of my parents' home and into an apartment, marked the beginning of a new life, a new job, and what would soon be a new relationship.

I was the first tenant in the new Country Club Towers in Clifton. My efficiency apartment was $105/month, which I could manage with what I was making with Rogers. Rogers and I made business trips together, played club matches in Cranford together, and went to tournaments together. Importantly, his luxury apartment on Lexington Avenue in New York allowed us to lead a bachelor's lifestyle on Friday nights and practice and play at Lawrence's table tennis club on 96th Street and Broadway on the weekend. It all seemed too good to be true, and time would prove that it was.

Very little was required of either Rogers or me to keep the business running and profitable. The company was essentially a cash cow for Rogers. After his mother and sister received their share of the monthly income, Rogers did with the money as he pleased—which meant living in the luxury apartment in Manhattan, buying expensive cars, gambling on the stock market, and making frequent trips to Las Vegas for gaming. My role, I finally realized, was essentially to be his table tennis practice partner and travel companion.

If anyone had the potential of a *divinely inspired* life, it was

Rogers Case. But it only lasted until Rogers' father died and he inherited his father's company and his fortune.

On July 11, 2004, during a trip to Rhode Island to visit friends Erica Peterson and her husband Ray, I contacted Rogers' sister Muriel who lived in Newport. I invited her to have brunch with me and Helga at the Viking Hotel. Rogers' son William happened to be visiting his aunt Muriel and he joined us.

During brunch, Muriel told us the story of Rogers' tragic ending. "Due to an 'unfortunate' set of circumstances, Rogers lost everything. In a desperate move, when he knew I was not at home, he let himself into my house and 'borrowed' my collection of John Singer Sargent paintings. In 1993, at the age of sixty-five, Rogers suffered a 'massive stroke' and died at the wheel of his car," Muriel said. She did not go into detail about the "circumstances" which proved "unfortunate" for Rogers, but from my experience of working with him for two years, they most likely had to do with technology eliminating the need for Transandean transposition brackets, the acquisition of Transandean's telephone system in Colombia by a competitor, treachery of "friend" Bill Lewis who made off with the plans for manufacture of Rogers' brackets, and, I believe, most importantly, Rogers being handed a gift of wealth which he squandered by living a reckless lifestyle—which was what he lived (and died) for.

Helga & Me, Rogers' sister Muriel and his son William.
Viking Hotel, Newport, Rhode Island. July 11, 2004.

BERNIE BUKIET II

BY 1962, I had made some friends in the table tennis community, less for my ability and level of play than for my continuing interest in and commitment to the sport.

World-class players Sol Schiff and Marty Reisman invited me to play exhibitions with them; Bernie Bukiet and I became friends. Bernie's life was a day-to-day struggle. I occasionally invited him to stay with me at my apartment in Clifton when he was uncertain about where to stay that night.

In the summer of 1962, Bernie suggested that he and I enter the Canadian National Table Tennis Championships held each year in Toronto during the Canadian National Exposition. Bernie had reasons for asking me, not the least of which was my 1958 Beetle, which meant transportation for him to Toronto and back—a 475-mile trip each way.

Because of the costs involved, I was cool with the suggestion for a while, but what Bernie lacked in language skills he made up for in persistence. Bernie was a survivor; he knew how to get what he needed, which, in this case, was a ride to Toronto and back. Bernie's persistence led to one of the most important *divinely inspired* events of my lifetime.

As soon as Bernie and I arrived at the venue, one of the players caught my eye immediately. She was not only a very skilled player (seeded #2 in the tournament), but she was also very attractive. Bernie said to me, "Dean, I must go practice. You go talk to that girl." She was just getting off the practice table, so I moved quickly, gathered my courage, and asked her if she would like to "hit a few with me."

She said, "Okay."

We engaged in some small talk. "What's your name? Where are you from?"

She told me she was living in Montreal but was originally from Hamburg, Germany. She asked where I was from. When I told her I was from New Jersey, she said, "I have an aunt and uncle living in Nutley; is that far from where you live?"

"It's close. I can see Nutley from my apartment. If you ever come to visit them, perhaps we can get together," I said.

"Sure," she said.

Later that day, I was sitting alone in the bleacher stands watching matches when something hit me in the back of the head. It was a precision-guided orange peel launched by Helga from several rows up. To me, this orange peel carried with it a subtle message: *I'm interested enough to talk again.* I bounded up the bleacher seats, sat down next to her, and we talked. I suggested that we take a stroll around the fair grounds. She responded, "I have matches today; how about tomorrow?" I agreed, and we spent a good part of the next afternoon together, deciding that we would meet again if she came to New Jersey.

On my next trip to Reisman's club, I asked a player named Marty Doss (with whom I had become quite friendly and whom I knew was from Hamburg) what he knew about Helga. Marty said they were in the juniors together and he didn't know much about her except that "she was always well-dressed and was always with her father." To me, what Marty had to say about Helga spoke volumes about her.

On October 1, 1962, I was excited to receive a letter from Helga with the news that she was coming to New York City on the weekend of October 6 to visit her aunt and uncle in Nutley, New Jersey. She was driving with friends who were coming to New York to visit friends on Riverside Drive, which was just blocks from Reisman's club!

Stunning! To me, this was clearly a series of *divinely inspired* events! Bernie persuades me to come to Canada, Helga and I meet, and Helga informs me that her aunt and uncle live less than five minutes from my apartment in Clifton. Now Helga's coming to visit them, arriving on Saturday, October 6, just blocks from Reisman's Club, at a time and place I would probably be in any case! You can't make this up, but *divine intelligence* can!

In December 1962, Helga made a return visit to Germany, during which she and her parents took a ski vacation in *Wintersportplatz*, Oberstdorf. Over a period of twenty-one months, Helga and I met in Montreal several times, arranged for meetings at tournaments, and exchanged correspondence.

After numerous 800-mile roundtrips to Montreal in my Beetle, and a flurry of correspondence, we gathered Helga's belongings and made a final trip to New Jersey on May 30, 1964.

Final trip to New Jersey on May 30, 1964.

MEL SCHNALL / JACK BRADY / PETER RENZO / CLEM BIANCHI

American Loose Leaf Staff

A SLUGGISH ECONOMY and, I believe, my relationship with Helga, upset my friendship with Rogers. He terminated our business relationship on January 5, 1964.

So, the year 1964 began with a mixed blessing; Helga and I were about to get married, but I was without a job.

On February 4, 1964, in response to an ad in the local newspaper, I was hired for a position in the advertising department of a company called Raybestos-Manhattan in neighboring Passaic. The salary was less than I was making with Rogers, but expenses were low. When I accepted the job, I was living at home, and commuting to and from my office was a ten-minute walk.

This month without a job was one of the few times in my life that I was out of work and had to apply for a job. By the grace of God, every other job opportunity during my sixty-eight-year career was offered to me.

With what I was able to put aside while working for Rogers, I made a down payment on a two-family house in Clifton. Toward the end of 1964, Helga and I moved into the downstairs rooms and rented the upstairs to two elderly sisters.

Being a catalog designer and print buyer at Raybestos-Manhattan soon became tedious—not very challenging or rewarding either mentally or financially. So I was receptive when one of my suppliers offered me a position. He was an elderly gentleman named John Orr, owner of a commercial photography studio, The Garraway Company. So, I left Raybestos-Manhattan on March 18, 1966, and joined the Garraway Company.

It did not take me long to realize that when I accepted John Orr's offer, I walked into a hornet's nest. Apparently the office manager, Nancy Cook, had been led to believe she would take over the company when John retired.

I don't know how she did it, but she wasted no time in getting me out.

Less than a month after I started, and one month after our first child, Eric, was born on March 5, 1966, I was again without a job. But what an unbelievable blessing this turned out to be!

A period in my life notable for "mixed blessings" now begins to unfold. In another event, *divinely inspired* in its timing and perfectly suited to my background, John Orr learned of an opening at one of his client's companies—a company named American Loose Leaf in Clifton—as a designer and manufacturer of loose-leaf binders. John recommended me for the job. I interviewed with the owner, Mel Schnall, and he hired me on the spot.

By the grace of God, I didn't miss a beat. Fortuitous in its timing, I replaced a man whom Mel had recently discovered was taking money under the table from his suppliers.

The job at American Loose Leaf also soon lost its luster, but I was again approached with an opportunity to make a move up—an opportunity I had to seriously consider despite the fact that it was coming from none other than Jack Brady, THE Jack Brady who, in 1959, drove Lou Kniep out of business by making off with 100 percent of his profitable accounts.

Since I'd last seen Jack Brady in 1959, he'd established a successful ad agency in Garfield, New Jersey. He came to American Loose Leaf for a meeting with me in December 1966 under a pretext of needing loose-leaf binders, but his real mission was to discuss a job opportunity with me.

The time was between Christmas and New Year's. Jack came

with bad news and good news. The bad news was that his uncle, George Paterson, had died on Christmas Day. George had been Jack's PR guy and helped him with one of his accounts, Sier-Bath Gear in North Bergen, New Jersey. The good news was (as it turned out) that Jack offered George's job to me.

Of course, I had reasons not to trust Jack, not the least of which was the way he'd treated Lou Kniep—making off with 100 percent of Lou's profitable accounts without uttering a word to anyone, including me, and just not showing up for work one day. Bingo! Lou was out of business and I could've been out of a job! But I also knew that, as he'd done in 1950, Jack would be doing whatever was in his best interest. If it happened to be also in my best interest, that'd be okay with him.

Jack's offer was too good not to consider.

The next day, I shared the news about Jack's offer with Mel Schnall. Mel came up with an amazingly creative counteroffer that I was comfortable with—to work for Jack part-time and for Mel part-time—and Mel would not reduce my salary, if I could keep up with the work!

So, my salary would more than double—from $12K/year to $27K/year overnight! Jack's condition was that I (and Helga) interview and be approved by Peter Renzo, VP of Sales at Sier-Bath Gear, Jack's largest account.

After some lengthy discussions with Helga, and some soul-searching, I told Jack that I was interested. Jack arranged for a brunch/meeting/interview for me and Helga at Peter Renzo's home in Saddle River, New Jersey, on Sunday morning, January 1, 1967. (Jack was an action guy.)

Peter was not only VP of sales and marketing at Sier-Bath, but he was also the brother-in-law of the president, Ed Bianchi.

Jack Brady

The interview was more of a five-star Sunday brunch at the home of Peter and Marilyn—with just Jack, his wife Florence, me, and Helga. Peter and Marilyn liked me, but they *loved* Helga—impressed by not only her good looks ("She looks just like Marlene Schmidt, 1961 Miss Universe," Marilyn said) but also the fact that she was a table tennis player and that she and I met at a tournament.

Jack Brady, in introducing me and Helga to Peter Renzo in 1967, set in motion an entirely new *divinely inspired* career for me as he did when he introduced me to Lou Kniep in 1950. In seventeen years, life had come full circle, with a third life-altering event, all of which can be traced directly back to three inspired relocations—to Scoles Avenue in 1935, to Katherine Avenue in 1942, and to Ricker Road in 1961.

During brunch, Marilyn casually mentioned that their niece, Terry Bianchi, had recently married a tennis pro from Upper Saddle River. The comment slipped right by me, but Helga picked up on it immediately.

"Are you the family that Frank Brennan married into?" Helga asked.

"Yes," said Peter, "we're part of the Bianchi family. I'm the brother of the wife of Ed Bianchi, president of Sier-Bath. Terry is his daughter." Helga knew of the connection because Frank's mother, Lillian Brennan, one of my mother's best friends, had invited my mother to the wedding, and my mother had shared details of the event with Helga. How *divinely inspired* was that connection?

In July 1971, Peter called me at my office at JA Brady when Jack was vacationing on Long Beach Island to inform me that there was some "unhappiness" with Jack's billing practices. He said he would talk to Jack about it when he returned, but he wanted to know if I would be receptive to the idea of joining Sier-Bath as their full-time Ad Manager.

This phone call was a *divinely inspired*, life-altering event. Realizing that Jack was about to lose the account, I quickly agreed on the spot to Peter's offer. The day after I was hired by Peter, with his permission, I backed up my car to the JA Brady office, gathered all the files I needed to do my job as ad manager, and loaded them into my car. The files were owned by Sier-Bath and I was now an employee of the company. I really had no choice in the matter since Jack was about to lose the account and, again, I would have been out of a job. This move was a bit unconventional, but as I learned as a pre-teen from the Dugan truck driver, "I'd rather ask forgiveness than permission."

My first assignment for Peter and Sier-Bath was to assist with an ASME event in May 1967 called the Spring Round-up, an annual get-together of about 1,000 executives of engineering companies.

I started full-time with Sier-Bath on August 16, 1971. I learned early that Peter was a table tennis fan, but I learned only later how a *divinely inspired* event played a role in Jack winning the Sier-Bath account.

The level of table tennis that Jack reached when he and I were playing every lunch hour at Kniep's earned him a position on the Passaic Knights of Columbus table tennis team and in a short time helped him become their best player. It was here that Jack met a Sier-Bath employee named Bruno Dorski. Bruno introduced Jack to Peter Renzo, who happened to be looking for an ad agency!

Not long after joining Sier-Bath, I found myself embroiled in a dispute between Peter and his twenty-nine-year-old nephew, Clem, Ed Bianchi's son. Ed, as we've learned, was president of the company and son of the founder Clementi Bianchi.

Ed had named Clem his potential successor. One of Clem's first missions seemed to be to downplay Peter's role in the company. The situation created a stressful environment for me. Both Clem and Peter began giving me conflicting assignments. My loyalty was to Peter, but Clem claimed he was acting on his father's behalf.

This dispute was a lose-lose for me, but in early 1974, Clem asked me to help him set up an ad agency, which would include the Sier-Bath Gear account for starters. I found it to be another offer I couldn't refuse! Clem had thrown the rabbit right into the briar patch!

Three generations of Bianchi's

Peter Renzo in 1970. Peter was ahead of his time.

Frank & Terry Brennan in 1969 & 1998.

BILL LECHLER I

ON TUESDAY, AUGUST 30, 1983, after arriving home late the night before from a family camping vacation in Cape Cod, I received a 7:30 A.M. call from Douglas Newton, president of Hansen Transmissions in Branford, Connecticut. Newton got right to the point. He wanted to know if I was available to have lunch with him and a man named Bill Lechler, his new marketing manager. The call caught me off guard because I hadn't heard from Newton since he became president of Hansen. Newton lived in Canada, and I knew that he had his own agency in Montreal. Nevertheless, following my rule of "just show up," I said I was available, and I was on the road before 8:30 A.M. for the 102-mile trip.

Following a short meeting in the Hansen conference room, Doug Newton, Bill Lechler, and I went to lunch at the Chowder Pot. Back at the office, Bill and I had an in-depth meeting, during which I agreed to propose an advertising and trade show program for the balance of 1983 and fiscal year '84.

On the following Friday, I mailed a package to Bill Lechler containing the proposal. I later learned that when Bill reviewed my proposal and budget with Newton, he was told that "there would be no money for advertising and trade shows, that you're hired to use your contacts and network in the power transmission industry and go out on the road and bring in orders." That led to a confrontation between Newton and Bill, and Bill was terminated—less than a year after he was hired.

When I called Bill to follow up on my proposal, Linda Ceruzzi, the receptionist, told me that Bill was no longer with the company. I was shocked and pursued the issue no further, knowing that Newton had his own agency in Montreal.

However, this was not to be the end of my connection to Bill Lechler.

Destiny was not to be denied!

On July 2, 1984, during a meeting with Peter Renzo at his office in North Bergen, Peter mentioned to me that two representatives of a company called ESCO Power (Sier-Bath's agent for couplings in Europe), Yves van Delft and Jean Delpire, would be coming in on July 12th to discuss the marketing of variable speed drives in the US. Peter had experience with Sier-Bath gears, gear couplings, and open gearing, but not with variable speed drives.

PRECISION GEARS · GEAR SYSTEMS
SIER BATH

Peter asked me if I knew anyone in the industry who might shed some light on this segment of the PT industry for him. Bill Lechler's name immediately came to mind, and I mentioned him to Peter; he asked me if I knew how to get in touch with him. I looked in my wallet, and lo-and-behold, I still had Bill's business card, which contained his home telephone number in Blue Bell, Pennsylvania. How this call unfolded was *divinely inspired*! It led to a life-changing experience for both me and my family.

I dialed the number from Peter's telephone and Bill's wife, Jane, answered. I introduced myself and asked to speak to Bill.

Not sure if he would remember me from our meeting at Hansen a year earlier, I reintroduced myself, introduced Peter, and told him that Peter was interested in talking to him about variable speed drives and marketing. Peter suggested to Bill that he come to North Bergen for a meeting. Bingo!

To help Bill become familiar with the Sier-Bath product line, I gathered a set of literature—Sier-Bath history and printed material—for him to study for the meeting. Helga and I then met him (and his mother) on Sunday, July 8, at our country club in Mountain Lakes.

What I learned from this meeting was that Bill was out of a job! His business card showed that he was a "Manufacturer's Representative."

At the meeting at Loews Glenpointe in Teaneck on July 12th, 1984, Bill made a presentation on the US variable speed drives market to Yves van Delft and Jean Delpire. Bill then had a follow-up meeting with Peter Renzo and me, during which Bill presented an invoice to Peter for his services. Peter flinched a bit at the amount. He handed the invoice to me and said, "sign this and put it in for payment." Peter congratulated Bill on his presentation, they shook hands, and Bill was on his way.

I believe Bill never forgot this meeting on this day.

It appeared for the second time that my association with

Bill Lechler would end, but for a second time I was wrong. On November 14th, 1984, at the suggestion of Peter, I accompanied him to a power transmission distributor's meeting in New Orleans. As we entered the lobby to register, the first person I happened upon was none other than Bill Lechler! I have no doubt that this meeting on this day in this place was *divinely inspired*! Bill told me that he had just been hired by a company "in your neighborhood," Sumitomo Machinery, and he invited me up to his hospitality suite. I wasted no time in taking him up on his invitation. His wife, Jane, was his gracious hostess.

Bill had a display of Sumitomo catalogs, which he showed to me with the comment, "they look to me like they could use some improving. Call me for an appointment when you get back to New Jersey. I'll show you the plant and we can talk about catalogs."

Me and Bill Lechler.

This trip to New Orleans was a *divinely inspired event* that would change the lives of me and our family forever!

On Thursday, December 13th, 1984, I took Bill up on his invitation to visit him at Sumitomo in Teterboro. Following a brief meeting with Bill, he suggested that I work through his advertising manager, Paul Pisano. I immediately called Paul and made an appointment to meet the next day.

(I learned something from nearly everyone I worked with—not necessarily from what they said but from what they did. I learned from watching Jack Brady, "when you see an opportunity, jump on it. Don't waste a split second!")

On December 14th, Paul and I met in a small conference room off the lobby, and for about an hour, I showed Paul samples of work I'd done, mainly for clients in the power transmission industry—Sier-Bath Gear, Hansen Transmissions, Voith Transmissions, and Torrington Bearing. Paul appeared to listen but didn't ask any questions. When I was finished with my presentation, he said, "We really don't do that much advertising." Only, as I learned later, about $750,000/year. "If we need something, I'll call you." With that, he showed me to the door.

Walking to my car, I thought, *Pisano's not getting away with blowing me off like this.* I returned to the lobby and told the receptionist I wanted to speak with Mr. Lechler. She got Bill on the phone, and I said to him, "I just had a meeting with Pisano, and he blew me off. If it's his decision about whether or not I have an opportunity at Sumitomo, I don't have a prayer."

Bill said, "Tell the receptionist to bring you into my office." To make a long story bearable, several months later, Bill gave Pisano an "opportunity" to work in sales. Then Bill and his office manager, John Cali, who was coordinating printing through Thompson Printing, and their salesman Jerry Bond asked me to quote on every catalog job that came up. Bill terminated his relationship with Sumitomo's New York ad agency and asked me to take over the $500,000 ad program. The Rubicon had been crossed! Life would never be the same.

Thanks to the good fortune of acquiring the Sumitomo account in early 1985—and the support of Bill Lechler—by the end of the year, our billings increased from less than $200,000/ year to more than seven-figures!

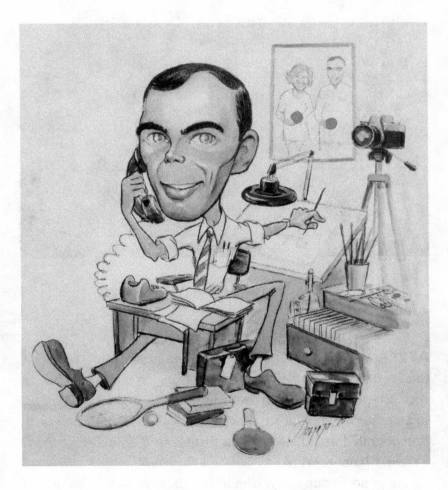

Caricature by Larry Trombeta

JOHN, MARY, LES, HELGA, & RAY

Mary Weber

AFTER WORKING OUT of our home in Kinnelon for more than two years, on April 17, 1975, we relocated our agency, along with our photostat and typesetting service called Photo Design, to an office building at 1250 Rt. 23 owned by friend Bob Ward. Bob operated an ad agency and printer in the building named Carelli, Glynn, & Ward.

As good fortune and *divine intelligence* would have it, I found at Carelli, Glynn, & Ward not only an excellent facility and compatible work environment, but three extremely talented and hard-working graphic artists who would eventually become colleagues and friends of mine and Helga's—John and Mary Weber and Les Scott.

In 1975, Mary and Les were employees of CG&W. In August of that year, I needed a slide presentation for Sier-Bath and I brought the project to CG&W to produce for me. I first reviewed the job with Bob Ward and his art director, Victor Jaskot. Victor then assigned the project to Les Scott for layout of the slides and to Mary for typesetting.

My first contact with Mary was related to that project. In August 1975, I reviewed proofs of the slides with her. Slide production at that time had to be created on "172 boards" with overlays for color, then photographed with a 35mm camera.

Helga

Later that year, Mary dropped in at my office to tell me that she was going into her own business and was looking for space from which to service her customers. I immediately offered her desk space and gave her one of her first jobs under the name of Type'N Graphics—a seating list for the 1976 ASME Spring Round-up, which she typeset on her IBM MTST typesetter.

The entire staff of Dean Johnson & Associates at this time consisted of Helga and me. All others were freelance.

Our agency could not have functioned without Helga. She exhibited persistence and skill as bookkeeper, media director, bill collector, and master of the Atlee Brown's Ad Agency computer system. Atlee's system was difficult for her at first, but she stuck with it and, over time, mastered it all in addition to raising three children, running a household, cooking, gardening, making time for her own tennis, and helping the kids with theirs, all of which allowed me the freedom to concentrate on servicing customers and coordinating the activities of Mary, John, Les, and Ray.

Soon after moving to the CG&W building, I began giving business to Bob Ward's Litho 4 Printers, which was also in the building.

One day, while going over a job with Jack Preis, the shop foreman of Litho 4, I noticed a set of "mechanicals" (paste-ups on 172 Illustration Board) on his desk. They were extraordinarily clean and professional, much in the style of Jack Brady.

I asked Preis who the artist was that prepared them. "Les Scott, an artist upstairs," he replied. It was the first time I had heard Les' name. I watched for an opportunity to speak with Les privately, then asked him if he would be willing to do some freelance work for me.

He said he was available. I started giving Les work during the day, which he would take home, work on at night, and often return the following day.

I could hardly believe my incredibly good fortune in meeting

Les, clearly a *divinely inspired* event. Les was trained as an artist in England. He was incredibly talented and provided me with an extremely valuable service. Les eventually left CG&W and started working with me, virtually full-time, as my freelance art director.

Les Scott

RAY JOHNSON

Brother Ray Built a Volksplane! This is how he did it. This is a photo I took of Ray airborne a few days after his maiden flight on July 5, 1978.

RAY GOT THE plans for this Volksplane from an engineer that worked for Boeing. When Ray saw the plans, he thought they looked like something he could do. It took him three and a half years to build, but it turned out to be a masterpiece of beauty and precision. He built it in his garage in Butler, New Jersey. Over 5,000 sets of plans were sold for this homebuilt airplane, but because of the patience, skill, time, and perseverance it requires, only a small percentage of those purchased actually ever became a reality.

When I saw it for the first time, somewhat in awe, I asked Ray, "How did you do that?"

Ray then launched into a lengthy description of the process. How is the fuselage held together? "With glue and small nails." Where did you get the four wing struts? "I made them." Where did the wheels and brakes come from? "Go-cart items. I bought them," he said.

He then continued, "A guy from Blairstown by the name of Al Butler was a big help to me with his knowledge and equipment. A relative named Vic Geronimo had a fabrication shop in Wayne who was also a huge help.

"The wings and rudder and elevator were also wood. The wings had two spars each, front and rear. Ribs attached to the spars gave the shape to the wing. The covering of the wing, elevator, and rudder was called Dacron. I covered the surfaces with it and applied heat to it and it shrunk, making a nice snug fit. There was also a process called rib stitching, which held the heated fabric to the wings.

"Then there was the engine and controls, which was challenging. I came across an ad from a guy in Texas that sold VW engines. He built them up from parts bought in Mexico. Cost me $475 plus shipping with the prop hub installed, which was a big plus. A friend named Norman Mege helped with the engine installation.

"The carburetor was from a motorcycle called a Posa. It worked great. A control cable into the cockpit opened and closed it. When I opened it, and when gas started dripping, I would turn the prop, and it usually started on the first spin. The prop was made especially for the counterclockwise rotation of the engine by a guy from Texas named Ray Hegey. I made the cowling myself with the fuel tank attached.

"It took me and Norman a while to get the right adjustment of the carburetor before it started with the tail tied to a rope to the garage door. After all parts were finished, I trucked it to Lincoln Park airport where I had an FAA inspection and the guy wrote out an airworthiness certificate."

Our uncle Vic was at the airport on July 5th, 1978. He called Ray and said, "the wind was right to take off to the north."

When asked how the flight went, Ray replied, "It flew great once the pilot got over the jitters."

Helga, who witnessed the maiden flight said, "I'm glad it's a single seater." One of the morals of this story is that no one, including Ray, can do it alone.

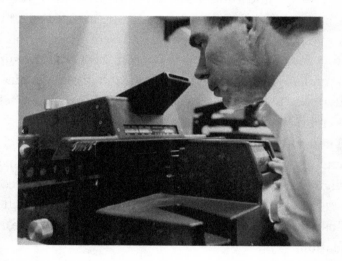

In the early 1970s, Ray applied his skills to the business of typesetting by setting up a business in support of John and Mary Weber at Type'N Graphics and my advertising business.

TED BLACK

In the photo above, I'm working with a genius named Ted Black (right), the most talented writer and photographer I've ever known, and his son, Fred. Ted and Fred were introduced to me by Bill Lechler to supervise the project.

SUMITOMO TRACES ITS roots to a bookshop in Kyoto, Japan, founded in 1615 by a former Buddhist priest, Masatomo Sumitomo. The diamond shaped Igeta logo is reminiscent of a type of frame placed over a well in pre-modern Japan.

The location of the Sumitomo plant in Teterboro was perfect for me—just a thirty-minute drive from our office in Kinnelon and within easy driving distance of my second largest account, Sier-Bath Gear, which was just ten minutes from Sumitomo. I could often call on both of them on the same day. A logistical miracle for me—I could not have planned it! Divine intelligence can!

Notice the portion of the building in the foreground in the shape of the Sumitomo Igeta (logo). This was offices and administration. The small, dark portion of the building was the "Igeta" room used for cafeteria, parties, and meetings. The largest portion of the building was gearbox assembly. An amazingly creative design based on a 400-year-old concept.

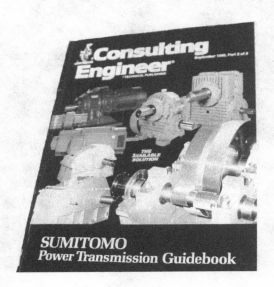

The single largest project I ever coordinated in my career was done for Sumitomo. It was reported in the trade press to be the largest ad ever placed in a trade publication—a 216-page insert in *Consulting Engineer Magazine.*

LES SCOTT

IN THE EARLY evening of Monday, October 30, 1989, Bill Berkenbush (partner in Boise Graphics, my printing pre-press service) called to give me the shocking news that his cleaning service had mistakenly disposed of five plastic bags of photographic chromes (8 X 10 color transparencies) and separations (films made from the chromes, including the retouching/dot etching of my customer's catalog). The Boise team had been working on this catalog for five months, and final films had already been approved by Cindy Vagel, Design House product manager.

This meant that all of the material for an entire fifty-two-page, four-color catalog had been inadvertently thrown in the trash! Time and material to reach this point in the project had been close to $100,000.

"I'm only calling you now because I've had everyone in the shop looking for your job all day. It's not here. It must have been thrown in the trash," he said.

"Let's call the garbage collector and find out what they did with the stuff," I said.

"I already did that. They dumped it in a landfill in Pennsylvania on Saturday; there's already two more days of garbage on top of it. Forget it!"

Cindy Vagel and Bill Berkenbush, co-owner of Boise Graphics on November 3, 1989. Cindy posed long enough for me to take a photo during the second check of her fifty-two-page, four-color catalog after the original material was inadvertently trashed.

The smiles are misleading; the pressure on this day was palpable. (Cindy's expression says: *watch out Dean, you could lose your house!***)**

"Who's going to tell Cindy?"

"I already did," said Bill. "She'll be calling you."

I no sooner hung up with Bill when Cindy called. "Bill told me what happened," she said. "I just talked to Jeff, my boss. He said, 'Tell Dean that if we don't have our catalogs in time for the sales meeting in Princeton on December 2nd, we are going to sue him for everything he's got, including his house!'"

Work on the Design House catalog had begun sometime in June 1989 at Mike Tesi Photography. Redoing the photography would be out of the question. My only hope was that either Mike Tesi or Les Scott (or both) had saved the "outtakes" (those versions of the photo setups that would generally be acceptable but were, in the opinion of Cindy Vagel, "marginal" for one reason or another).

First thing Tuesday morning, I called Mike Tesi and explained the situation. Mike said he did have some of the outtakes. I then checked with Les and he also had some. A thorough check of all the outtakes revealed that we had at least one 8 X 10 chrome of every photo in the catalog, albeit some "marginal" in quality.

Bill, and his partner Gerry Hartline, had begun pre-press work soon after the photography had been completed in late September. Everything they had done in the previous month would have to be re-done in about a week to give Greg Jordan and his team at Teagle & Little time to print, bind, and ship the job by late November.

Bill and Gerry and their team worked around the clock with Cindy looking over their shoulder 24/7. Everyone involved, including Greg Jordan and his team at Teagle & Little, did an unbelievable job in getting copies of the catalog to the Scanticon Hotel in Princeton in time (and on budget) for the Design House sales meeting—and taking off my shoulders the most stressful, potentially disastrous situation I had ever encountered in my business career.

For us, the job was profitable; for Billy and Gerry, not so much. At a lunch meeting to celebrate the successful completion of the job, Cindy Vagel informed Billy and Gerry that Jeff, owner of Design House, wanted to be compensated for the additional time that Cindy had to spend checking the second round of separations—$12,000.

Cindy had given me a heads-up about it, so I watched Billy's face for a reaction. His eyeballs disappeared! All I could see were the whites of his eyes. His face was ashen, his body went limp, and he crumbled off his chair to the floor in a dead faint.

The good news for us was that by the grace of God, the job was completed on time, on budget, and profitably. The catalog won design awards and we continued to do yearly business with Design House.

My secret to the successful conclusion of this near-disastrous events was that I never lost faith in Les Scott, Bill Berkenbush, or his team. I believed in the adage: *when fear enters, let faith in.*

A MARRIAGE MEANT TO BE

OUR MARRIAGE, WHICH started with a *divinely inspired* meeting at a table tennis tournament in 1962, has lasted more than sixty years. This meeting was no accident; it was meant to be. Helga is the mate that fate had me created for. Whenever I'm asked the secret to the longevity of our marriage, I respond, "There is no simple answer. It starts, I believe, with a strong common interest, which, in our case, is table tennis and tennis. Add to that a set of common values—in Helga's case, European 'old world' values and in my case, values derived from grandparents Anna and Fred Johnson, both of whom had an enormous impact on my upbringing."

HELGA'S PARENTS ERIKA AND HEINRICH BÜLTEMEIER

WHEN WE MARRIED, Helga's parents did not know who I was and I did not know them, but when we met in 1965, Helga's mother and father could not have been more gracious and accepting of me. During our first visit to Hamburg, they welcomed me with open arms, as did all of the Bültemeier family.

Their acceptance was immediate and unconditional. How fortunate, how *divinely inspired* it was to become a member of this wonderful family.

I felt more fortunate than anyone can imagine. I could not have felt more excited in meeting them than if I had hit the lottery.

The capacity of Helga's parents for giving seemed to be unlimited, and their expectations for receiving seemed not to exist. From 1965, when Helga and I visited Lokstedt together for the first time, to 1969, when Heinrich and Erika visited our home in Kinnelon for the first time, to their last visit to Virginia Beach in 2000, and Helga's last visit to Lokstedt in 2010, many wonderful, exciting visits were exchanged in between.

Helga, her parents, and her brother Jürgen are the most generous people I've known.

HEINRICH BÜLTEMEIER

Heinrich played table tennis into his nineties.

DURING THE WINTER of 1973, I was invited by Heinrich to ski with him in Austria. I flew to Munich, where I met Heinrich, and we drove 300 kilometers to the Hochschober Hotel in Türracher Höhe in Austria.

At the Hochschober was a maître d' named Peter. When he greeted us for our first meal, he expressed his gratitude to us and said how pleased he was to have us as his guest. Addressing Heinrich in German, he said, "And we have many nice young ladies for your American friend." With perfect composure, Heinrich replied with a smile, "He is my son-in-law."

In his career, Heinrich was an engineer; he specialized in bridge building, which was a skill in great demand following the war. He took me on a tour of his plant in Hamburg where he was Chief Engineer in charge of more than 200 engineers. He was fluent in three languages (German, English, and Polish). He was a skilled athlete. In college, he participated at a high level in the 150-year-old tradition of fencing and competitive horseback riding, and he competed in four World Table Tennis Veterans Championships and won medals in his nineties.

JÜRGEN BÜLTEMEIER

JÜRGEN BÜLTEMEIER IS among the most thoughtful, most generous, most caring, and most giving individuals I've ever known, other than his sister, Helga, and his parents, Erika and Heinrich. I am blessed to have been a member of the Bültemeier family since 1964.

Jürgen had a long and distinguished career in the Hamburg Police Force which started in January 1962 as an officer and which included teaching at the German Police Academy for twenty years. He continued his service until his retirement as the Chief Commissioner of Hamburg.

Jürgen also had a noteworthy career in his participation in the sport of table tennis. In the 2002/2003 season, he won the Men's Singles, Men's Doubles, and Mixed Doubles in the highly competitive Hamburg Championship. By the way, Jürgen's sister, Helga, was winner of the 1955 and 1956 Hamburg Junior Championships.

Jürgen was a member of the Niendorfer TSV (Turn—und Sportverein) for over seventy years; twenty-two of those years, he served as a volunteer at NTSV.

> *To: Dean Johnson & Jürgen Bültemeier.*
> *In recognition of their participation in the 13th World Veterans Table Tennis Championships, the 15th of May, 2006, in Bremen, Germany. Dean was a guest of Jürgen.*

SIEGFRIED HOH

SIEGFRIED HOH WAS a student-friend of Helga's father, Heinrich. Siegfried's wife, Elsa, was Helga's godmother. Sig died in October 2015 at the age of 100.

In 1969, another *divinely inspired* event was initiated by Helga's "uncle" Siegfried Hoh. It turned out to be life-altering to our family. Sig was transferred from his job as a physicist with IT&T in Nutley, New Jersey, to Cape Canaveral, Florida. Sig and his wife Elsa tried renting their home, which they had built in 1964 in Kinnelon, but being "absentee landlords" was not working out for them for a variety of reasons.

During one of our occasional trips from Clifton to Kinnelon to check on the Hoh's house while it was vacant, Sig met us there and took the opportunity to suggest that we buy it! We willingly and readily accepted.

After a successful effort to sell our house in Clifton, in April 1969, we moved to this beautiful, solidly built home, with a pond and a barn on six wooded acres in the mountains of northern New Jersey shown on the next page.

Another year of incredible good fortune and *divinely inspired* events was 1969. It was the year in which Curtiss-Wright Corporation opened a property they owned in Kinnelon for employee recreation, named Lake Rickabear, to Kinnelon residents.

Lake Rickabear, just a five-minute drive from home, was not only a lake but a gated recreational complex which included walking trails, a putting green, tennis courts, and a clubhouse— all supervised by a wonderful man named Bill Callahan.

Eventually, during the summer months, Helga spent nearly every day at the lake with Eric, Karen, and Kristina; Helga brought their lunches there, they made friends there, they learned to swim there, and we entertained family and friends there. It was also within walking distance of a beautiful park named Silas Condict. This move was a blessing!

The most important feature of the lake for our family, however, were the tennis courts. Many years of table tennis experience taught us fundamentals of "stroke production," how to compete, and how to win. We had a "jump" on others who were caught up in the 1970s tennis explosion. In addition to practicing and competing at Lake Rickabear, our playing network extended to Park Lakes Club and Rockaway River Country Club where we also made friends and competed.

Helga, the children, and I lived here and enjoyed this home
and its surroundings for twenty-five years.

Helga and me at Lake Rickabear in 1971.
Photo by Ray Johnson.

As Helga and I learned more about the fundamentals of tennis, we taught the fundamentals to Eric, Karen, and Kristina. All three attended local tennis camps, tennis groups, and, in the summer, Frank Brennan Tennis Camps. Eric and Karen had summer jobs as tennis counselors at tennis camps. Karen worked for eight summers as a counselor at Carlos Goffi's Tennis Camp in Florida.

Eric, Karen, and Kristina all went on to play college tennis, and we became the only family ever to field three teams at the Equitable Family Tennis Challenge at the US Tennis Open in Flushing Meadow in 1984—Helga and Eric, me and Karen, and Helga and Kristina. We qualified by winning eight rounds in district and sectional matches.

Karen has since been coach of the Middlebury College Women's Tennis Team and, in 2016, was men and women's assistant tennis coach at Pacific University in Portland, Oregon.

All of this was made possible because of the *divinely inspired* event in 1969 when Siegfried Hoh asked me and Helga a simple question: "Would you like to buy our house?" The lives of all of us were then changed forever.

CBS News sent their sports reporter, Joe Zone, to Kinnelon on September 3, 1986, to interview Kristina and Helga on qualifying for the main draw of the Equitable Family Tennis Challenge at Flushing Meadow.

Helga and Kristina competing at Flushing Meadow.

BILL DOLWICK

Bill with self-portrait January 25, 1971. Photo taken by me.

IN 1971 JACK Brady had a client named Associated Pile—a manufacturer of Point Protectors for use on pile drivers.

One day, Jack asked me to run an errand for him, to bring a job to one of his clients, Jack Dougherty, vice-president of Associated. This was not unusual; I was an Account Exec at Jack's agency. During a casual conversation with Jack Dougherty, he asked me if I knew anyone in our industry who was a portrait artist. A fellow player at my table tennis club named Bill Dolwick came to mind. I did not know Bill well at the time, but I had heard that he was an artist.

Jack Dougherty said he was looking for someone to do a portrait of his wife's father. Her father was no longer alive, so Jack said, "the portrait will have to be created from a collection of small photos from old family albums."

"It's going to take an artist with special skills to do this, Jack," I said. "But I'll look into it for you."

During my next table tennis practice session in Fair Lawn, I asked Bill Dolwick if he would like to "hit a few with me." Following our hitting session, I told Bill that I had heard he was an artist and asked him what his specialty was. He said portraits. Bingo!

I told Bill that a client of mine, Jack Dougherty, vice-president of a company in Clifton, was looking for a portrait artist, and I asked him if he would be interested in talking to him. Bill said he would be. I gave Bill Jack's contact information and he and Jack got together to discuss Jack's needs.

During our next practice session, I learned from Bill that Jack Dougherty was interested in a portrait of his father-in-law. Jack gathered for Bill a selection of old photos of his father-in-law from which Bill could be guided to create the portrait.

I later learned that Bill had attended the Cleveland Institute of Art where he received the Gotwalt Scholarship for a painting of his grandfather. He matriculated at the Slade School of Art for two years. When he returned from England, he envisioned selling his portraits, but he didn't sell enough to make a living, so he became an illustrator and worked for Illustration House, a company in New York. His paintings became legendary. After several years, he was elected into the New York Society of Illustrators and remained a member until his death in 1993.

It turns out that Bill was a world-class portrait artist. How fortunate! How *divinely inspired* was this?

Bill finished the painting and delivered it to Jack in a relatively short time.

Bottom line, Jack Dougherty and his family were so pleased with the result that, according to Bill, Jack ordered ten more paintings for other members of his wife's family—which meant more than a year's work for Bill.

When the project was completed, Bill offered to do a portrait of me and Helga, which he did in 1973. The painting was in color, of course.

We have had the pleasure of this beautiful, world-class portrait hanging in our bedroom for forty-eight years, just because one day I happened to be available to fill in for Jack Brady at one of his accounts.

Interestingly, for our portrait, Bill apparently used a technique for creating a painting of photographic quality with just a paint brush, such as the artist Johannes Vermeer did in the mid-1600s.

To create the astonishing effects of light and shadow, Vermeer used a camera obscura—a box with a hole in it. The inside of the box was painted white and, using a series of lenses and mirrors, it reflected the outside image within. This intensified the light and shadows of the reflection, allowing Vermeer to see finer detail of proportions.

Helga and I sat for Bill as he photographed us with a white background, studio lighting, a 2-1/4 X 2-1/4 Rolleiflex camera, and black-and-white film. He called us again to his studio to give us a choice of views from his proofs.

I was not there to witness first-hand his next step, but I assume Bill selected the negative from the print we all approved, converted it to a positive transparency, and projected the image onto his canvas to guide his brush strokes. The result was a painting with a level of quality rivaling ones of presidents that hang in the White House. A priceless gift to us from one of America's great portrait artists—just because I agreed to "sit in" for a few minutes at a meeting with one of Jack Brady's clients, which, considering the unique circumstances under which this story unfolded, was clearly, to me, a *divinely inspired* event.

Ten years earlier, I instinctively used basically the same
technique as Bill did—and tools with which I was familiar
(photography and a sharp #2 pencil) to create this series of
sketches of table tennis legends Dick Miles, Marty Reisman,
and Erwin Klein.

ERIC JOHNSON

There is wisdom in the old adage "haste makes waste."
But when we are faced with what we are absolutely sure
is a golden opportunity, not a moment can be wasted.

YET ANOTHER *divinely inspired* event occurred in April 1984
when a clerk in the admissions office of Guilford College in North
Carolina mistakenly sent our son Eric an acceptance letter to the

school (rather than the rejection letter the admissions office had decided upon).

We received the acceptance letter on April 9, 1984. We had done some research on Guilford. We knew that the school would be a good fit for Eric, but we were also aware of the high academic standards of the school, making it a "long shot" for him. We were all pleased when Eric received the acceptance letter. I decided immediately that, on the pretext of touring the campus, it would be a good idea to confirm it in person.

On April 11, Eric and I flew to Greensboro. We were waiting outside the admissions office when the door opened.

When I told the admissions director who we were, it was clear she knew exactly who we were, and she looked horrified. She explained to us that the acceptance letter had been sent in error and that the correct rejection letter was already in the mail! She said we were free to tour the campus on our own until it was time to go to the airport for our flight back to New Jersey.

I protested and asked to meet with the Guilford tennis coach, Ray Alley, who already had a copy of Eric's tennis credentials. Ray Alley was also appalled by the error of the admissions office and asked Eric if he would be willing to "hit a few" with some of the members of his tennis team. Eric did well against all of them, so the coach had a meeting with the Admissions Director and persuaded her to give Eric an interview. Again, to his credit, Eric did well and was accepted to Guilford on the condition that he improve some of his grades at Delbarton. The decision by the clerk in the admissions office to send an acceptance letter was proven right. Eric was qualified to attend Guilford. His performance on the tennis court and his second interview with the Admissions Director proved it! He is now the Elementary Director of the very prestigious Raleigh School, an independent pre-school.

By the way, Eric met his wife, Maria, at Guilford College. If we had not moved quickly, if I had waited even one more day before traveling with Eric to Guilford, Eric's marriage to Maria and the birth of their two beautiful daughters, Isabel and Camille, could never have happened! But destiny would not be denied!

JOHN & MARY WEBER

Mary and John Weber, in 2010, standing in the parking lot of what was, in 1985, the Stonehouse Inn. The building in the background is the one in which our offices, in 2021, are still located.

IN 1985, A man named Ron Vigneri (one of my tennis doubles partners) was in the process of converting indoor tennis courts he had built on Kinnelon Road to office condominiums. The location was close to our home in Kinnelon and not far from offices we were renting at the time in the CG&W building on Route 23.

On May 14th of that year, another man named Ron Franks invited John and Mary Weber (who were our tenants at the time) to lunch at the Stonehouse Inn next to the building Ron Vigneri was converting to condos. Ron Franks had proposed to John and Mary that they join him (as tenants of his) in space he planned to buy in Ron Vigneri's refurbished facility.

Mary, very thoughtfully and out of consideration to me, suggested I might also be interested in hearing what Ron Franks had to say, so I joined them.

When I realized what the meeting was about—that I was at risk of losing John and Mary as tenants in the CG&W building, in which we shared office space, and losing the proximity of their services—I was appalled.

I promptly excused myself (hinting at a bathroom break) and sprinted across the few yards from the restaurant to Ron Vigneri's building in the hope that he would be there working with his father. I was breathless as I searched the building for Ron. By the grace of God, I found him. I asked him to quickly show me what other space he had available.

Ron Vigneri showed me a suite of offices, which looked perfect for us. I told him, on the spot, that I would take it. (A commitment of nearly $100,000.) I then hurried back from my "bathroom break" to the lunch meeting in time for Ron Franks to invite us next door to inspect the space he was offering to John and Mary and from which I had just returned.

After looking at the space Ron Franks was offering, I said to John and Mary, "Let's look at what else is available." The space to which I had just committed, Suite #12, looked good to them also, but when Ron Franks inquired about it, Ron Vigneri said, "Sorry, that space is taken." (Thankfully, Ron Vigneri did not mention the fact that it had been taken only moments earlier, by me.)

When we returned to our office, I asked John and Mary what they thought of #12. They both said they liked it. To their shock and surprise, I then told them that I had just given a verbal commitment to Ron Vigneri to purchase it.

The following day, John and Mary and I agreed on a partnership to purchase the space together, which we did on October 17.

On October 25, 1985, Dean Johnson and Associates, Type'N Graphics, and Photo Design moved their offices to 170 Kinnelon Road.

Now, more than thirty-seven years later, the four of us still own the space, and it has been a good investment.

I credit that investment not just to my timely "bathroom break" but to Mary Weber's thoughtful, in my opinion, *divinely inspired* invitation to join her and John in the meeting with Ron Franks.

GREG JORDAN

ON AUGUST 15, 1988, while our family was vacationing in Virginia Beach, I visited Greg Jordan, president of a printing company in Norfolk named Teagle & Little. My purpose in being there was to identify a printing company with whom I could work and trust to handle a very significant amount of printing which I would be bringing from my current printer, Jersey Printing, in Paterson, New Jersey.

During our meeting, I explained to Greg that I had a client, Sumitomo Machinery, which was relocating from New Jersey to Chesapeake. I explained to Greg that the point of the meeting was to discuss with him the printing of Sumitomo catalogs. I told Greg that I controlled nearly $400,000/year in catalog printing and that I was in possession of the negatives required to make the plates—that I had retrieved all the negatives from my printer in New Jersey and, at the moment, they were in the trunk of my car.

Greg responded, "I already have a salesman calling on Sumitomo in Chesapeake, and he should probably be entitled to any business they could obtain there." He called the salesman, who happened to be in the office, and Greg called him into the meeting.

The salesman said that he had made sales calls on Dawn Ranges and Judy Hrushka in Sumitomo's temporary office in the Armada Hofler building in Chesapeake and that they had promised him an opportunity to quote on printing once the company was settled in their new location in Chesapeake.

I explained to Greg's salesman that Bill Lechler, the president of Sumitomo who I work with directly, has given me the authority to purchase printing, and I'm sure that Dawn and Judy have no purchasing authority, nor will they have.

Greg then asked me if he could have a few minutes alone with his salesman. When I returned to Greg's office, Greg said, "I believe what you said, and I will work directly with you on the printing of Sumitomo catalogs." This decision by Greg, I believe, was *divinely inspired*. It was life-altering for me.

This was just one of the many blessings that Greg was responsible for during our more than thirty-year relationship. He also introduced me to our publisher, John Koehler.

Greg's "leap of faith" in me resulted in several million dollars in printing business for Teagle & Little over the next thirteen years.

"There are many talented people who haven't fulfilled their dreams because they overthought it, or they were too cautious, and were unwilling to make the leap of faith."
—James Cameron, filmmake

DR. KEN JEWEL

When consciousness is "fragmented," it starts a war in the mind-body system. This war lies behind many diseases, giving rise to what modern medicine calls the "psychosomatic component." The Rishis call it "the fear born of duality," and they would consider it not a component, but the chief cause of all illness.

—Deepak Chopra

ON A BLISTERING-HOT August 20, 1989, following two doubles matches with tennis partner Mike O'Donnell at the Mountain Lakes Club, then a Heineken at home and a nap on our reclining chair, I awoke with a pain in my buttocks which felt like I had been beaten with a baseball bat! This episode would morph into severe sciatic pain *which would last for more than two years.*

A week later, the pain in my back was so severe, I had to default a friendly tennis match with Greg Jordan at the Virginia Beach Racquet Club.

Pain episodes then started to become more frequent and more intense. I tried in vain to suffer through it, probably in denial about the severity. Not until the following January did I seek professional relief. I first tried chiropractic—a female chiropractor in Norfolk who, after two months of treatments, offered no relief from the constant pain.

On April 3rd, 1990, I made an appointment with a local orthopedic surgeon in Virginia Beach to whom I was referred by Bill Lechler. During a follow-up visit on May 19th, 1990, based only on an x-ray, he recommended surgery. "The sooner the better," he said. When I pushed back, he added, "If you don't have it done immediately, you will come back to me on your hands and knees begging me to do it."

Meanwhile, continuing to take weekly flights to Chesapeake, I tried various back supports and corsets, which offered no relief. I tried alternating ice and heat on the sacroiliac joint, and I joined a local spa in Kinnelon for weekly whirlpool baths and started an exercise regimen. Nothing helped. It all just seemed to make the pain worse.

To add to my stress, on May 1, 1990, on the recommendation of her doctor, I admitted my mother to Passaic General Hospital for blood tests to determine why her energy level was low. Thinking she'd be coming home that day, she didn't even bring toilet articles with her, so I went home to retrieve them. One test led to another, one week to another. When I was not in Chesapeake, I visited Ma daily in the hospital.

In the midst of it all, on June 7th, Ma's brother John, one of my favorite uncles, died. I reluctantly gave the sad news to Ma. The first half of 1990 for me was one stressful event after another.

I continued to search for relief from what was now chronic, debilitating pain. In June, I tried another chiropractor in Pequannock. After several treatments by him, I experienced no relief.

On July 31, 1990, three months to the day after she was admitted to Passaic General Hospital, Ma passed away—apparently due to an infection. I lost my strongest supporter, my best friend.

December 1990 brought a bit of a breakthrough in my back issue. Just on an impulse, I visited Park Lakes Tennis Club in Mountain Lakes one day. A tennis friend named Ken Jewel, who owned a radiology lab in Caldwell, asked me where I'd been. "We miss seeing you here, Dean. What's going on?"

I told him about the chronic pain I was experiencing and about the many unsuccessful attempts at finding relief.

"Here's my card. Call my lab. Tell Peggy I told you to make an appointment. I'll do an MRI myself and I'll call you with the result," he said. Ken did the MRI on the 10th. A few days later, he called me with encouraging news: "I don't see anything going on here that should be causing you this kind of pain. I suggest you give it time. If it doesn't get any worse, be patient; if it does get worse, call me." It was good to know that, apparently, I wasn't dealing with a structural issue like a herniated disc. But I continued to search for relief.

The following day, in desperation, I made an appointment with a doctor who had an office in my building. He made an appointment for me at Chilton Hospital that day. There he gave me a painful Depomedrol epidural and assured me that the pain would be gone "by tomorrow." Not true; it offered no relief at all.

Again, I was confined to bed applying ice packs to my sacroiliac joint every three hours for three days. On the advice of a friend, I tried a medication called Hydrocodone synthesized from codeine. It only served to make me ill.

Having tried pain clinics, medication, and doctors offering no solution for nearly a year-and-a-half, I began to get desperate. I started to dwell on the hardships and pain and uncertainties that my grandparents Anna and Fred must have endured to get here to this country in the nineteenth century—about the patience, persistence, and perseverance they both exhibited in not only getting here and surviving here, but flourishing here, and how Anna studied her Bible daily and relied on her faith for strength. Keeping them in my thoughts gave me hope. I began a series of daily exercises prescribed by Leon Root in his book *No More Aching Back*. As painful as they were, I was faithful with the exercises for several months.

At Helga's suggestion, in April 1991, I tried one more doctor, Reinhard Schwartz, recommended by friends of ours, Adam and Elfie Pataki. Following a one-hour exam, he had no other suggestion but to refer to his brother who had a condition similar to mine; he became pain-free only after he divorced his wife! So much for Dr. Schwartz!

In June 1991, I was recommended to a physical therapist named Dan Meyers in Kinnelon. Whether he was the right guy at the right time or if my condition had just begun to run its course, his treatments, almost immediately, began to offer some relief. I started regular treatments and exercises with Dan on June 8th. By the 18th, I was able to start traveling again to Chesapeake— not to go to the plant, but to have my friend and Sumitomo's customer service manager, Marcel Zapatero, meet me at Comfort

Suites to go over assignments. The entrance to my room was adjacent to the parking lot, to save me steps getting to it.

On October 19th, 1991—while walking across the parking lot of Rockaway Mall on the way to a movie—Helga looked at me and said, "You're not limping." That moment signaled the end of my painful experience. After two years, the sciatic pain in my leg was suddenly gone!

At that moment, I felt my faith was justified. I had never lost faith in the belief that God would somehow get me out of this mess. That's not to say I was never afraid. But when I felt fearful, I let faith in.

Through it all, I never lost faith, nor did I forget Dr. Jewel's opinion: "I don't see anything going on here that should be causing you this kind of pain. I suggest you give it time. If it doesn't get any worse, be patient." I believe that the impulsive, unplanned visit to the Park Lakes Club in December 1990 was a *divinely inspired* event. Although the pain continued after my chance meeting with Dr. Ken Jewel, it never got any worse, which encouraged me to be patient.

BILL LECHLER II

ACUTELY AWARE OF the pain and pressure I was under, Bill Lechler, now president of Sumitomo, made an offer to me I could not refuse—to buy my business, pay for our relocation, and hire me as a full-time marketing communications manager. I saw Bill's offer as a long-term win-win. This turned out to be an incredible, *divinely inspired* offer!

After discussions with Helga, I responded to Bill in the affirmative. Bill then instructed his sales manager, Steve King, to prepare a "package" for me which would detail the verbal agreement Bill and I had made.

King stalled and dragged his feet from May 1992 until January 1993, at which time I wrote and mailed a strong letter to Bill, detailing King's delay for which I knew Bill would have no patience.

Bill replied, "I read King the riot act."

Bill knew what he was getting—my experience, my loyalty, and my work ethic. I believe he had also not forgotten the day in July 1984 when I approved his invoice to Peter Renzo for consulting when Bill was out of a job.

King finally completed and presented to me a "package," which I signed on February 4th, 1993. I then rented a house in Norfolk and started full-time employment at Sumitomo on March 2nd. Thus began a new phase in our life and the start of discussions between me and Helga about relocation to Hampton Roads.

Having lived on Ricker Road in Kinnelon for twenty-five years, we were well-established. We loved our home, which had been designed and built by Helga's uncle Siegfried Hoh. It was a unique structure, as strong as a bunker, on six wooded and rocky acres in the hills of western New Jersey. Our office was there. Helga's friends were there. Tennis was there.

For good reason, Helga was very reluctant to relocate. I argued that without the income from Sumitomo, what then? Helga's question was, "Can't you find another Sumitomo?" My question to Helga was, "How do I find another Bill Lechler?"

My good friend, Bill Lechler, died on July 31, 2017.

Our home in Kinnelon was designed and built by Helga's uncle Siegfried. It had the strength of a bunker on six acres atop a massive monolithic rock and adjacent to a 270-foot deep well which provided an unlimited supply of pure drinking water. We loved it. It was painful to leave it.

DECK JORDAN

Deck coaxing a duck out of the pool.

THROUGHOUT MY CAREER, I became friends with business associates that I liked. If they also happened to be in a position to buy my services, so much the better. Renzo at Sier-Bath, Lechler at Sumitomo, Ilgner at Gestra, Arning at Supradur, Humphrey at Hansen, Magee at Sumitomo and Bonfiglioli, Zapatero at Sier-Bath, Sumitomo, Hansen, and David Brown—all friends. The same was true of my vendors, like Greg and Deck Jordan.

I believe that the most important habit I developed in my career was to genuinely work on behalf of both customers and vendors to create win-wins that generated profits and income for both.

Deck Jordan was the founder of Teagle & Little, my most

reliable source for printing of Sumitomo catalogs. Deck was also a good friend. I house-sat Deck's home in Norfolk from March 9th, 1993, until relocation from Kinnelon to Virginia Beach on November 23rd, 1994. Renting Deck's home was a win-win for both me and Deck, since Deck was now spending most of his time in Florida and Exuma. Deck was happy if I just kept the house warm in the winter and the pool clean in the summer.

On July 4, 2020, my good friend Deck Jordan passed away at age ninety.

Born in Dalton, Georgia, in 1929, Deck spent most of his formative years in Wilmington, North Carolina, where he learned the printing trade. At the age of twenty-five, he purchased a small printing company in Norfolk—Teagle & Little—which grew into one of the premier printing companies in the Southeast. Clients throughout the years included the White House, Lexus, Audi, and many other nationally recognized companies.

Deck had a love for sailing which included multiple crossings of the Atlantic in vessels he purchased. During one of his journeys, Deck experienced some very rough conditions and took refuge on Great Exuma, an island in the Bahamas. He built a home on one of their beautiful beaches where he lived for more than twenty years.

In my opinion, Deck Jordan was a borderline genius; it was a pleasure and, I believe, a *divinely inspired* event to have met him and known him.

Deck lived a life most people dream of. We hope he finds the same joy in his new home.

What was disastrous news for us at Sumitomo in 1987 turned into a life-long benefit for our family in 1994.

And Deck Jordan was largely responsible for that.

Deck's house in 1994.

"DJs" prepared for a night out in 1994.

JANICE KUYKENDALL

FROM THE DAY in 1993 when I moved to Norfolk until the day I alerted Helga to come south to look at a home I found for sale in Virginia Beach, I searched on my own, and Helga made monthly visits and appointments with local real estate agents, looking for a place in which to settle in Hampton Roads. For nearly two years, I was unsuccessful in finding the right house in the right location at the right price.

In September 1994, I received a call at my Sumitomo office from Janis Kuykendall, an agent with whom I had earlier contact about a home in Virginia Beach. I loved the house, but it was way out of our price range, and it had since been taken off the market.

Janice called to tell me that the house was again on the market at a much-reduced price; the owner had had a buyer, but the deal fell through at the last minute. Meanwhile, the owner had already bought a home in Florida and was now in a bind with two mortgages. Janis did not forget me; she went the "extra mile" in alerting me.

"We have to act quickly," Janice said. On September 25th, Helga and I met with Janice to look at the house. When we finished the tour, Helga whispered to me, "I could live here." I breathed a huge sigh of relief! The nearly two-year effort was paying dividends!

Helga and I wasted no time in making an offer to the owner. He accepted, and on November 24th, 1994, the day before Thanksgiving, we moved to Virginia Beach.

I left Deck Jordan's home, which I had been renting since March 2nd, 1993. We also brought the contents of the self-storage space we had been renting in Chesapeake to Virginia Beach. Done!

How *divinely inspired* was this? At the very moment that the owner was desperate to sell, we were even more eager to find a home in a location, in a style, in a size, and in a price range Helga and I would find acceptable. On this day, the stars were again aligned perfectly for us!

Today, looking twenty-five years into the rear-view mirror, the Sumitomo relocation to Virginia could not have been more fortuitous nor more timely for us.

Our home in Kinnelon was built with the strength of a bunker on six acres atop a massive monolithic rock; we loved it, and it was painful to leave it.

As much as Helga would have loved to stay in Kinnelon, living in semi-retirement in Virginia Beach has its advantages—a more moderate climate without losing the four seasons, three blocks from the oceanfront, a state park for walking and swimming in the bay, a short walk to the post office, the bank, the doctor, and a pharmacy, six supermarkets and a mall within easy drive, good hospitals close by, tennis for Helga, table tennis for me, year-round entertainment at the beach and in Norfolk, and Pungo in southern Virginia Beach for strawberry and peach farms and beautiful parks and rivers close by.

We could not have planned it more perfectly.
Divine intelligence could!

MIKE BABUIN

IN JULY 2008 I was invited by table tennis friends Tim Boggan and Dick Evans to be a member of the US Table Tennis Hall of Fame Board of Directors to fill a vacancy created when long-time board member Mary McIlwain passed away on March 25, 2008. This invitation, which came out of the blue, created the next seamless link in my chain of *divinely inspired* life events.

For the next several years, my primary contribution on the board was to create PowerPoint presentations of inductees into the USTTA Hall of Fame, which are presented at the Hall of Fame dinner held during the US Nationals in December. I was also asked by Tim and Dick to be part of a three-member committee which selects potential inductees. Dick was President of the USTTA Hall of Fame; Tim played the most important role in selection, preparation, and distribution of potential inductee resumes.

With Dick Evans and Tim Boggan during the 2010 Nationals in Las Vegas.

Being a member of committees like these expanded my exposure and network in the table tennis community—a network which included a man named Mike Babuin.

On October 18, 2010, Mike called me to ask if I had heard that Virginia Beach had submitted a bid to host the 2011 US Nationals. This one call set in motion yet another chain of *divinely inspired* events that would forever alter the direction of my life and smooth the transition to the next stage of my career, as more and more of my clients retired or changed jobs.

The next morning, I called a fellow named Buddy Wheeler at the Virginia Beach Convention and Visitors Bureau. I told him I had heard about the bid he was making and gave him a summary of my background.

Buddy invited me to his office to discuss how I could be

helpful to his team in making a presentation to the USATT Board of Directors at the 2010 Nationals in December. During the meeting, Buddy "recruited" me to be their table tennis "go-to" guy for the presentation.

For the next month-and-a-half, Buddy and I (and two other highly professional sports marketing representatives on his team, Matt Robinette and Nancy Helman) worked on the PowerPoint.

In December, at the USA Table Tennis Board of Directors meeting, Buddy made the presentation; on January 10th, the board met and voted in favor of Virginia Beach to host the 2011 Nationals. This was huge!

Soon after the announcement, Mike Cavanaugh, USATT CEO, appointed me to serve as Chairman of the Virginia Beach Local Organizing Committee. The efforts by me and other members of the committee, namely Mike Babuin, were successful and, for the first time in thirty years, the US Nationals would be held at a location other than Las Vegas!

On March 16, 2012, Tim Boggan, Dick Evans, Mike Babuin, and I held a meeting during the Cary Cup tournament to discuss the possibility of identifying a location and creating a USTTA Hall of Fame Museum. Dick, Tim, and Mike asked me to serve as Chairman of the Committee.

After Mike and I showed this proposed museum photo of table tennis legend Sol Schiff to Ann Campbell, owner and president of Triangle Table Tennis, she gave the green light for us to produce ten more framed, matted, and captioned photos of our twelve table tennis "legends" and display them on a thirty foot wall at Triangle Table Tennis along with displays of Hall of Fame plaques of inductees, Lifetime Achievement Award recipients, and display cases of artifacts and memorabilia.

Donna Sakai, President of the US Table Tennis Hall of Fame, cut the ribbon to mark the opening of the USTTA Hall of Fame Museum at Triangle Table Tennis in Morrisville, North Carolina, on March 21, 2015. As Chairman of the Museum Committee, I was Master of Ceremony for the event.

The positive role that Mike Babuin has played in my career and personal life is beyond measure. I believe that Mike was *divinely inspired* to do what he did for me and for the sport of table tennis.

MARTY REISMAN

Action photo of Marty taken by me at Mr. Lawrence's place on 96th St. Camera is a 4 X 5 Speed Graphic mounted on a tripod lighted by dual high-speed flash.

NEVER IN MY wildest dreams could I have imagined leading the blessed life I did, enjoying the lifestyle I did, and becoming friends with the fascinating people I did. Only through the miracle of *divine inspiration* could my life have unfolded the way it did.

Marty Reisman was one of the four world-class players about

whom I read in Coleman Clark's book on table tennis in 1957.

My friendship with Reisman spanned more than fifty years. Knowing him was a glimpse into the mind of a genius, although there were times when I wasn't sure if I was dealing with a genius or a crazy person.

Early in our friendship, Marty said to me, "I can never recall not playing good table tennis. My racket became a delicate and a sensuous connection between the ball and my brain. The more I used it, the more dependent I became on my racket, until I was madly in love with this incredible instrument."

Posing with table tennis legends Sol Schiff, Dick Miles, Lou Pagliaro, and Marty Reisman during a get-together at Dick Miles' apartment in 2007.

Hungry for competition, Marty found his way to Lawrence's Table Tennis Parlor on Broadway where some of the best players in the world hung out, practiced, and competed with each other. In just a few years, he became a world-class player, having honed his skills against the best players in America for money, fame, and talent. His love for the game eventually lured him away from the Lower East Side of Manhattan, shattering his mother's dream that he would become a doctor. Ida the Yenta, a next-door neighbor, revels with satisfaction that her prediction—"Marty will grow up to be a bum just like his father"—was right on the money.

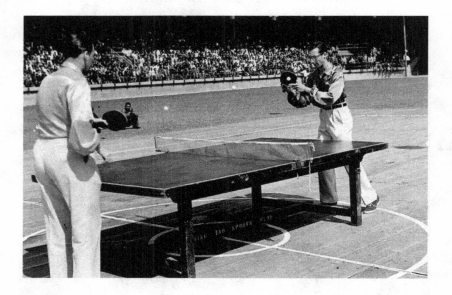

But few people have had a life as diverse, glamorous, and packed with adventure as Marty Reisman.

For two years, in the early 1950s, Marty toured the world as a star attraction with the Harlem Globetrotters, performing half-time exhibition table tennis matches with his partner, Doug Cartland, and appearing before a total (Marty's estimation) of more than ten million fans.

In the Spring of 1975, I arranged with Marty to play an

exhibition at Kinnelon, at New Jersey High School, a very successful effort to raise money for the children of a neighboring family, the Knapps, whose parents, brother, and grandmother died in a fire at their home on Christmas Day, 1974. It was very generous of Marty to contribute his time.

In exchange for contributing his time and talent to the exhibition in Kinnelon, I produced a promotional brochure for Marty which included the design of a logo of which he made good use for more than thirty years. In the photo above, he's displaying the logo proudly.

Published by *Vault* and written by Ray Kennedy in the article titled, "A Little Night Music," the author describes Marty's table tennis game.

> For Marty Reisman, winner of 17 national and international table tennis titles—and hundreds of big-money bets—the performance served a different need. Like many professional gamblers, he insists that neither the pay nor the play is the thing. Rather, he says, it is the risk, the intrigue, the danger that exhilarates. "Though I need it to get the adrenaline flowing, the money is nothing, the excitement everything," he says. "I never

played a game for fun in my life."

Spoken like a true gunslinger—or is that the wily hustler talking? One can never be certain about a 'mythic figure,' which is what Tim Boggan, editor of bimonthly *Table Tennis Topics*, recalls of Reisman.

"No one plays with the same classical élan,: says Boggan. "No one carries the same aura. And no one for sure dresses the same as Marty Reisman. He adds dignity and class to a game that has no dignity and class. Yes, there is the cat burglar side, but he is a Cary Grant cat burglar, the kind of person who operates on both sides of some laws and makes it all seem right because he does it on his own terms. There is no comparable bravado figure in the game today. He is the James Bond of table tennis."

Also highlighted in Kennedy's article is the quote by Murray Kempton which declares, "To come upon Reisman is like finding some perfect specimen of a lost classic age, thin as a blade, the step a matador's, the stroke a kitten's."

Visit https://vault.si.com/vault/1977/11/21/a-little-night-music to read the beautiful article about my dear friend Marty Reisman.

Quoted in *Marty Reisman, A Retrospective, Volume I*, Howard Jacobson said, "Enter the prize fighter, Marty Reisman, hot from taking bets on himself in Lawrence's Table Tennis Parlor on Broadway, once a speakeasy owned by Legs Diamond and still not a joint where you threw challenges around lightly. And all at once the neon lights went on and the band started to play Gershwin" (*The Independent*, June 2000).

Marty told me that he believed he was "wired properly at

birth to play table tennis. I'm living the purpose for which I was born." And I couldn't believe him more.

Marty and I prior to their fundraising exhibition at Kinnelon, New Jersey High School, in 1975—proceeds to the Knapp family

When Reisman picks up his custom-made paddle and stalks toward a table, a murmuring crowd starts to form. He hits a few casual strokes, warming up. He's thin—137 pounds on a six-foot frame, his shoulders packed with tiers of muscle, as if engineered for flight (*Marty Reisman: A Retrospective, Volume I*).

Pencil rendition of Marty by me, 1963

Marty had legions of friends and admirers—many of whom claimed to be "Marty's best friend." But Marty called me on September 25, 2012, to confide in me that, "sometime after midnight this morning, I felt sick and in pain. I called a cab to take me to the emergency room at Beth Israel Hospital. I'm there now, Dean."

I spoke with Marty at every opportunity after that until, as a result of complications following open heart surgery on December 1, a little more than ten weeks after he was admitted, Marty passed away on December 7, 2012.

DICK MILES

1963 pencil renderings of Dick by me.

BRUCE WEBER'S *New York Times* article "Dick Miles, Record-Setting U.S. Table Tennis Player, Dies at 85," did a marvelous job highlighting Dick's life and his career. The article can be found online at https://www.nytimes.com/2010/10/24/sports/24miles.html. Below are some of my favorite sections, in which the author displays Dick's table tennis abilities.

Weber outlines Miles' biography as follows:

Richard Theodore Miles was born in Manhattan on

June 12, 1925, and was raised by his mother, Ivy. By the time he was a teenager, he was playing table tennis ten hours a day or more.

After high school, he briefly attended New York University, but mostly, from then on, he just played table tennis. His signature stroke was a potent forehand using an underhand grip (that is, the racket head pointed down). Beginning with a looping backswing with the forearm held close to his body, he finished with a snap of the wrist that delivered the ball with astonishing topspin and speed. It was his strategy to drive the ball to the center of the table.

"Instead of hitting to the wings, he hit to the middle," Mr. Boggan said. "He'd go for the gut again and again."

Over the years, Miles supported himself by playing exhibitions and creating trick-shot shows (for many years, he traveled with the U.S.O., performing for American troops abroad). . . . He was also the author of a 1968 primer, *The Game of Table Tennis*, and in the 1960s and 1970s, he was a contributor to *Sports Illustrated* magazine. . . .

A lifelong New Yorker, Miles met Mary Detsch in 1970 in Central Park. Companions for 40 years, they married in 1993. She is his only immediate survivor. "We met because he had a cute dog," Ms. Detsch said in a phone interview. When he told her he was a table tennis player, she said, "I thought, 'What could that possibly mean?' I soon found out. It's its own culture. We traveled all over the world together, and he had table tennis friends everywhere."

Dick and me at Dick's apartment on August 7, 2006, the day I presented Dick's Retrospective to him. Photo by Dick's wife, Mary Detsch.

PARADISE TENNIS

Me and friend Rogers Case, Paradise Island, Bahamas, 1963—playing not table tennis, but Paradise Tennis, which is played on an oversized table with larger rackets and balls. Photo by Tom Donohue.

WHEN I ASKED Dick Miles to what he would attribute his success in table tennis he said, "I worked very hard on my game, but I really, really hated to lose."

Paradise Tennis is a game invented by Huntington Hartford, heir to the A&P fortune, owner of Paradise Island, and a regular at Reisman's Riverside Table Tennis. Hartford changed the name of the island from Hog Island to Paradise Island because, as he told me one night, he planned to upgrade the island to a tourist resort with a yacht marina, an amphitheater, a golf course, and a hotel.

Paradise Tennis is played on a table nine feet wide, eighteen feet long, and twenty-eight inches high. The surface is aluminum painted green. The net is a foot high. Tennis racket-sized paddles with short handles are used. The ball is about the size of a tennis ball.

The first time I saw "Hunt" at Reisman's after returning from a trip to Nassau he said, "My caretaker, Tom Donohue, told me you visited Paradise Island. How did you like it?"

"My friend and I loved the tour that Tom and his wife gave us, but even more, we appreciated the opportunity to play your Paradise Tennis. What a thrill that was for us. Could you tell me a little, Hunt, about the tournament you held on Paradise Island?"

"I couldn't attend myself," he said. "I was on my way to Europe. But my friend Wendell Niles reported to me that the tournament was very exciting. All the 'greats' were there—Ellsworth Vines, Don Budge, Pancho Gonzales, Jack Kramer, Althea Gibson, and, of course, our friend, nine-time US National Table Tennis Champion Dick Miles.

"Wendell told me that the most exciting match of the tournament was between Pancho and Dick in the semis. Gonzales hit with his usual graceful style with lots of spin and was trying hard to win. But everything he hit came back.

"The few times Pancho tried to hit the ball hard, it just kept coming back. It was like hitting against a wall," he said.

"Miles said that when he played table tennis, he looked forward to long rallies, because after a while, he became 'at one' with the ball."

"Dick beat my friend Wendell Niles in the finals," Hunt said. "Niles had eliminated Kramer to reach the finals, while Miles beat Budge in the other semis. In the finals, Dick was too steady for Niles, and he won the tournament four and zero. Althea Gibson won the Women's, beating Nelle Longshore in the final three and zero."

1960s Dick Miles. Photo courtesy Marty Reisman.

Paradise Island fifty-seven years after Paradise Tennis tournament was held here. Huntington Hartford's dream of it becoming a tourist resort was realized when the Island was bought by Merv Griffin in 1988 for $365 million.

A REQUEST FROM DICK MILES

WHAT SEEMED TO be a simple request from friend Dick Miles turned out to be a historic day. Dick asked me to help bring together what would probably be the last historic legend get together at his apartment on Riverside Drive in Manhattan. It was too challenging, he said, for Sol Schiff, who lived in Brooklyn, and Lou Pagliaro, who lived on Staten Island, to make their way to Dick's apartment on their own.

On Sunday, October 14th, 2007, Helga and I drove from Virginia Beach to Staten Island to pick up Paggy, then to Brooklyn to pick up Sol, where he had been relocated from the Bronx to his niece's apartment.

In an ironic twist, these players, Marty Reisman, Dick Miles, Sol Schiff, and Lou Pagliaro were exactly those legendary players that I read about in Coleman Clark's book in 1957—the $1.25

book (and the players) that attracted me to the sport nearly sixty years ago to the day and changed my life!

After a wonderful get-together with friends, we took Sol back to Brooklyn and Paggy home to Staten Island, then returned to Virginia Beach on Monday. A 755-mile round trip. What a trip it was!

SIR HAROLD EVANS

IN 2001, BRITISH Journalists voted Harold Evans the "All-time greatest British newspaper editor."

Sir Harold was Editor of the *Sunday Times* and President of Random House. He was Knighted in 2004. (Sadly, Marty had passed away on December 7, 2013, and Sir Harold died on September 23, 2020.)

On July 18, 2013, I was invited by my friend Sir Harold Evans to his apartment in Manhattan to join in a tribute to our mutual friend Marty Reisman. The basement where the tribute was held was the scene of many friendly matches between Harold and Marty.

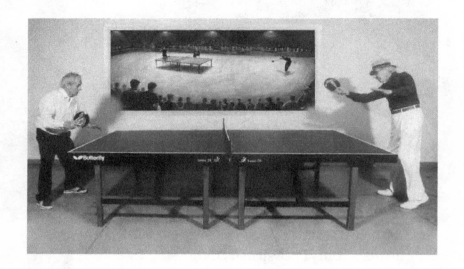

Painting on the wall is a depiction of Marty stroking his ballet-like backhand chop against Dick Miles during the 1949 US Open finals (*Marty Reisman: A Retrospective, Volume I*).
Painting by Mal Russell.

DEXTER GREY

DEXTER GREY IS infinitely more accomplished on piano keys than he is at a ping-pong table, but he and his twin brother Neal were worthy opponents for Marty Reisman and me at the 2007 US Nationals.

In Mylah De Leon's article, "Dexter Grey: Rebellious Audacity And Improvisations Highlight Latest Concert," published by *Asian Journal*, De Leon exerts, "Maestro Dexter Grey has mastered the piano . . . like no other performer of his genre. . . . While in China recently, he connected the East and West in an acclaimed performance."

Marty and I played Dexter and his twin brother Neal in an over-seventy doubles match on December 21, 2007, at the US Nationals in Las Vegas.

THE ERWIN KLEIN / SI WASSERMAN CONNECTION

Erwin Klein 1960s pencil rendering by me

USA TABLE TENNIS' biography of Erwin Klein says it best. The following can be found at https://www.teamusa.org/USA-Table-Tennis/History/Hall-of-Fame/Profiles/Erwin-Klein.

> Erwin Klein . . . four-time US Men's Singles Champion and (with Leah "Ping" Neuberger) 1956 World Mixed Doubles Champion—has been a legendry name in US table tennis for decades . . . literally ever since that US Open day in 1952 when, as an unranked, red-haired,

freckle-faced, fun-loving, "chubby" kid from a California playground, he forced Dave Krizman, US Boys #1, into a tenacious five-game final.

The backbone of table tennis in the Southern California area for many years was Si Wasserman. He served as President of the SCTTA from 1952 to 1955. His diligent work and enthusiastic avocation of table tennis was recognized by the national body when he was named executive vice president of the United States Table Tennis Association.

For the most part, Wasserman elected to stay in the background, giving advice and support to the energetic Ben Wollman, president of the local association. During many hectic controversies—sponge, antisponge, and so on—he could always be counted on to discuss and give judgment in a quiet, dignified manner, thereby gaining respect from both sides.

Wasserman's expert tutoring has helped develop many top players in this area—Erwin Klein, Leonard Cooperman, Sharon Acton, Charleen Hanson, and others. He has kept the Hollywood Table Tennis Center open on Highland Avenue, even on an unremunerative basis so that the players would have a place to meet and practice.

Most players do not know of the headaches and work that enter into a successful table tennis program. They would recognize Si's worth only if his support was missing.

Si Wasserman was chief executive from 1952–1955, the longest tenure of any CTTA president.

During this period, under Si's tutelage, Erwin Klein won his first major tournament, the Southern California Men's Singles, in February 1952. Erwin then went on to win the Canadian National Boys' and Junior Men's singles titles, the first of twenty-two national and international crowns he was destined to win.

Me & Si at the 2007 US Nationals

NORBERT VAN DE WALLE

Norbert competing in the 1961 Men's NTCs in Detroit where his record was 13-2.
Photo by Mal Anderson.

ONE OF THE often-told stories about Norbert is his extraordinary performance at the 1962 Nationals in New York is an event I can report first-hand since I was a participant and spellbound observer.

I first met Norbert at the '61 NTCs in Detroit.

The *USA Table Tennis* profile, on https://www.teamusa.org/
USA-Table-Tennis/History/Hall-of-Fame/Profiles/Norbert-
Van-de-Walle, displays Norbert's winnings.

> At the 1962 Nationals, he ousts [Chuck] Burns, 19
> in the 5th. Afterwards plays an incredible 23-21 in the
> 5th semi's match against Bobby Fields. For 90 minutes,
> it was heart-throbbing . . . Play became even more
> pulsating when Van de Walle suffers leg cramps. Bill
> Marlens reportedly comes out to minister to him. . . .
> Though Bobby led 19-14 in the expedited 5th, Norby is
> able to win this match, as Pauline Somael says, on sheer
> guts. Photos show that Fields, on losing, flings his bat to
> the table, then exchanges a sporting hug with Norby. . . .
> Listening to as many Frank Sinatra recordings
> whenever and wherever he could, Norby has been going
> off on USO Tours with his friend [Dick] Miles. They
> visit such faraway places as distant from one another
> as Vietnam and Alaska where the weather outside is 55
> degrees below zero and inside in the exhibition hall 80
> degrees above. At least once, Dick tells me, they think
> their plane is going down, and exchange stiff-upper-lip
> partings.

Norbert and me at the 2004 US Nationals.

FRANCK RAHARINOSY

ON JULY 3, 2013, I responded to an e-mail calling for someone to play the part of a "Reisman-like" character in a short editorial film. "Must live in Los Angeles or nearby. If interested e-mail photo by 5:00 P.M. pacific time today."

Of course, I didn't live in Los Angeles and had very little idea what an "editorial film" was about, but to me, it had the potential of a once-in-a-lifetime opportunity. What was the worst that could happen? A trip to LA, if it didn't work out. At the very least, I can set up an interview with Erwin Klein's daughter, Ava, for my Erwin Klein retrospective.

Our daughter Karen and her husband Jacob happened to be visiting. I asked Jacob, a skilled photographer, to come with me to my table tennis club meeting that night to take a few photos for the response to the e-mail about playing a Reisman-like character.

A few days later, I received a response from someone named Bon Duke, telling me that I had been chosen for the role and that the shooting would take place on July 22nd and 23rd and to please arrive on the 21st and plan to depart on the 24th. A follow-up email from Bon Duke asked me to let him know the hotel at which I would be staying so he can send me a "call sheet."

Photo I submitted was an attempt to simulate Marty's forehand.
Photo by Jake Wells.

What I didn't know was: what the film was about, where it would be shot, what my role in it would be, where I would stay in LA, how I would get to and from the airport, how I would get to and from the shooting location, what I would do for meals during my stay, and who is Bon Duke?

But I followed my instinct to "just show up."

I still did not know where the film was to be shot. I needed to know in what neighborhood to look for a hotel.

But on the 21st, I headed to Newark Airport. At this point, I believe Helga thought I had lost my mind.

I was at the gate when I received an e-mail from someone named Zoe who asked me to send her all my sizes—shirt, trousers, hat, shoes, and jacket. This was my first indication, with some relief, that someone was actually expecting me in LA.

When I arrived, I went directly to baggage claim where a man approached me and asked if I was Dean Johnson. More relief!

The man was my chauffer! He brought me to the Standard Hotel where they greeted me like a celebrity! They put me up in a 5-star room in the Standard which was the hotel at which the film would be shot. They had a wardrobe ready for me to try on and they covered all my expenses.

On the 22nd, I just hung out, relaxed, and chatted with the cast and crew.

Shooting on the 23rd was long and intense. The film crew was about half-a-dozen people—a producer, cameramen, lighting folks, sound folks, make-up artists, stylists, etc.

The story line, packed into two-and-a-half minutes, was about a young (twenty-something) ping-pong hustler who was making a few bucks working low-end clubs in LA. He was given a heads-up that the real money was in the high-end clubs downtown.

When the young hustler showed up at the Standard, he immediately recognized an old-timer hanging out whom he knew he would have to face. Finally, the time arrives for the showdown with the "old Master." Following a series of long, challenging rallies, the screen goes black with no indication as to who has won the match.

In the final scene, the young hustler and the "Old Master" are at the bar. The "Old Master" pats the hustler on the shoulder and says, "nice match," then takes the neatly rolled wad of cash from the hustler and walks out of the club.

What followed was the most difficult part of the two days for me—take after take after take of long rallies hitting the ball as hard as I could in the "match" against this young hustler. I was eighty-one; if I had not kept myself in shape, I would never have lasted through this part of the shoot.

The young hustler finally misses a ball completely and the screen goes blank.

I later learned that Franck Raharinosy who played the young hustler was behind the selection of me for the part of the "Old Master," dating back to the e-mail I received on July 3, 2013, paving the way for this *divinely inspired* event in my life.

STELLAN & ANGIE BENGTSSON

STELLAN BENGTSSON, WORLD CHAMPION

STELLAN BENGTSSON, AT eighteen, was the 1971 winner of the Worlds Men's Singles Championship over Shigeo Itoh in Nagoya, Japan. The photo at left, I took during a 1971 exhibition when Stellan played his friend Kjell Johansson at Madison Square Garden in New York. The photo was on the front cover of the July/August 1971 issue of *Table Tennis Topics* magazine. I have no idea what motivated me on that day in 1971 to drive the twenty miles from my home in Clifton, New Jersey, find parking near Madison Square Garden, pay the entry fee, and position myself close enough to the action to take this photo.

The photo at right is a bronze statue of Stellan which stands in front of the Falkhallen in Falkenberg, Sweden. I also took this photo in May 2018. There are some similarities in the figures—the body rotation, balance, the position of the left foot in the follow-through, the open palm of the right hand. I'd be honored if the sculptor of Stellan's statue was guided or inspired in any way by my 1971 photo.

In May 2018, I traveled to Falkenberg, Sweden, in order to attend meetings related to WVC 2018 to be held in Las Vegas for which I was an organizing committee member. The meetings in Sweden were held during the World Team Table Tennis Championships 2018 being held in Halmstad, Sweden.

While in Sweden, I stayed at the Grand Hotel in Falkenberg. While at the hotel, I read with interest in a promotional brochure that Falkenberg is the birthplace of Stellan Bengtsson. Stellan and I were on the WVC 2018 committee together, so we were acquainted.

I e-mailed Stellan to tell him that I was staying in a hotel in the town of his birth. "Be sure to visit my statue in front of the Falkhallen," he replied.

I asked the clerk at the desk for directions to the Falkhallen. It was just a five-minute walk. I immediately walked there to take a photo of the statue from an angle that looked best to me.

When I got home, I compared it to the photo on the front cover of the July/August 1971 issue of *Table Tennis Topics* magazine (which I had saved for forty-seven years).

I was blown away by the coincidental facts that (#1) I was one of the few officials working at the tournament held in Halmstad, housed at the Grand Hotel, (#2) that I learned by chance that Falkenberg was the birthplace of Stellan Bengtsson, (#3) that I learned from Stellan himself of the existence of his statue in front of the Falkhallen and was urged by him to visit it, (#4) without having my 1971 photo to guide me, I coincidentally took a photo of the statue very similar to Stellan's stroking position, and (#5) in 1971, it was nearly unheard of for me to travel from New Jersey to Madison Square Garden in New York to take a photo of a table tennis exhibition.

How *divinely inspired* it was for me to take these two photos and find an appropriate use for them forty-seven years after I took the first.

With friends, Dr. Herbert Neubauer and Hans Westling, and the famous bronze statue of 1971 Worlds Men's Singles Champion Stellan Bengtsson, taken in front of the Falkenberg Sports Center during the World Table Tennis Championships 2018, in Halmstad, Sweden.

Stellan, in addition to winning the Men's Singles title at the World Table Tennis Championships 1971, has won three World Championships, seven European Championships, sixty-five International Championships, and seven English Open titles.

Angie and Stellan conduct a highly successful table tennis camp in San Diego, California, called Stellangie Table Tennis. "We try to give every student the feeling that we are their personal coach," I once heard Angie say. "We're an inspiration, especially to our younger students. Many of them consider us their second mom and dad."

Angelita's biography, outlined by *Team USA* at https://www.teamusa.org/USA-Table-Tennis/History/Hall-of-Fame/Profiles/Angelita-Rosal-Bengtsson, describes her life story. Below is an excerpt.

> Angie (from her hometown San Diego) went to her first USOTC's (in Detroit) at age 11, in 1967.
>
> In both 1968 and '69—with Patty Martinez, Wendy Hicks, and Heather Angelinetta—she was on the winning USOTC team.... Angie won the '68 U.S. Open Girls U-13 . . . [and] in '69 and '70 she won the U.S. Open Girls U-15—first from Pam Ramsey, then from Judy Bochenski. . . . In '73, at the U.S. Open . . . [Angie] won the U-17 Girls Doubles with Judy, [and] the U-17 Mixed Doubles with Eric Thom.

In '79 Angie . . . played in her 13th consecutive U.S. Open. [In] '83 . . . Angie went to Sweden to train . . . and by 1985 had married 1971 World Champion Stellan Bengtsson.

In 1996, Angelita was inducted into the USATT Hall of Fame.

PATTY MARTINEZ

1969 - 2019

Photos by Mal Anderson

IN DECEMBER 2014, at the US Nationals in Las Vegas, I was waiting alone on the platform for the Monorail to bring me to the Convention Center. Suddenly, a young lady appeared. I said, "Hi, my name is Dean." She said, "Hi, I'm Patty Martinez." This was the first time I met Patty. I knew who she was, but I had never met her. What I subsequently learned about Patty is that she and my friend Marty Reisman are geniuses at the ping-pong table; *their brains were wired properly at birth to play ping-pong.*

Patty Martinez USA Table Tennis History Hall of Fame bio outlines her table tennis capabilities, along with how she got to be so successful. Below are some excerpts from https://www.teamusa.org/USA-Table-Tennis/History/Hall-of-Fame/Committee.

> Patty Martinez has been called a genius at the ping-pong table —her brain was apparently wired properly at birth to play ping-pong. She has a quick, "off-the-bounce," close-to-the-table game which make her unpredictable and keeps her opponents off-balance. Any ball on the forehand side is met quickly and decisively with precise forehand . . .

She shares these qualities with Marty Reisman, of course. Yet, a major difference in their games, however, is that if Marty is driven back from the table, he exhibits an impenetrable, graceful defense. Patty refuses to be driven back from the table; she has a good backhand block, but for the most part, her offense is her defense.

This instinctive strategy, at a very early age, brought Patty National titles not just in the Juniors but in Adult events in both the U.S. and Canada and selection to the U.S. team.

Patty is renowned for her 1965 U.S. Open finals match against 9-time Woman's champion Leah Neuberger—which she won at age thirteen!

. . . In 1961, when Patty was just 9, her father entered her in the1961 San Diego Open, at which she won the Women's Championship. It was at this tournament that Patty defeated Millie Littlejohn who held the Women's Singles title for a number of years. It was also at this tournament that her father realized that his daughter had the talent to be a future National Champion.

At 11, Patty won the 1964 U.S. Open junior championship and moved up to the women's division. She was little more than a curiosity when she arrived at the 1965 U.S. Open in Detroit—where she won the U.S. Women's title.

The genius of Patty is that she developed a unique set of table tennis skills on her own—with little formal instruction, without a coach to guide her stroke technique or strategy; she was guided by her own instincts. No one taught Patty her forehand, her backhand, the importance of footwork or the level of composure that saw her through some of the most dire of circumstances that would cause others to fold.

"I couldn't understand why anyone thought that what I was doing was so special. It just seemed natural to me. I couldn't understand why anyone couldn't do what I was doing," said Patty.

I knew Leah Neuberger very well. We traveled to tournaments together and competed together in New York-area Mixed events.

I liked Leah, and I have great respect and admiration for her achievements and contributions to the sport, especially as our historian. Leah was extremely bright; she had tremendous determination and worked hard on the fundamentals of her game, but I don't believe she blazed new ground in the sport as Marty and Patty did.

Leah and her sister Tybie's games sprouted and flourished as youngsters and, in Leah's words, "We were both very competitive. We drove each other to higher and higher levels of play, and we always had the advantage of having a built-in practice partner." Both Leah and Tybie won World's Mixed Doubles Championships—Tybie with Dick Miles in 1948 and Leah with Erwin Klein in 1956.

Both Patty and Marty are extremely intelligent. Their personalities, combined with a composure which belies an almost obsessive desire to win, make both of them winners, but also, at times, causes both to be as unpredictable and full of surprises as they are at the ping-pong table.

Patty went on to win two more US Opens, three National Junior titles, three Canadian National titles, and a three-time membership of the US Team to World Championships.

Today, in 2021, Patty continues to win National titles in her age group and Open titles in hardbat events.

I was blessed to have the opportunity to gain firsthand insight into the lives and talents of two of the greatest female players in the history of women's table tennis—Leah Neuberger and Patty Martinez.

Photo taken in 2015, when I won O80 doubles and Patty won O50 Doubles.

GEORGE BRATHWAITE

GEORGE'S ONLINE BIOGRAPHY, from which I've gathered the information below, can be found at https://www.georgebraithwaite.com/about/.

I've summarized his words, edited them for clarity, and added extra content.

George was born and raised in Georgetown, Guyana.

As a boy, he was athletically active and participated in a variety of sports such as cricket, soccer, cycling, and track and field, excelling especially at cricket and track and field.

Eventually, George move to the United States to further his education, and through a United Nations employee, he was invited to watch the UN play a cricket match. That day, the UN team was missing a player and needed a substitute. George did well, so at the suggestion of the team captain, he applied for a job at the UN, took the statistics examination, passed, and begun working at the UN that same year.

Coincidentally, shortly after joining the UN, George found an old hard rubber ping-pong paddle stored among some documents. He practiced hard. His table tennis career had begun! He then joined a team which had been formed at the UN to play other teams in New York. A member of the team happened to be Leah Neuberger. We had become friends by that time, and she invited me to play on the team. I don't remember connecting to George during that time, but in later discussions, we realized we had been playing matches at the UN at the same time, during the late 1950s.

In a few short years, many honors were bestowed upon George.

- He was selected by the United States Table Tennis Association (USTTA) as a goodwill ambassador to Central America where he played exhibition matches and coached.
- On his website, he says, in addition to all of this, he also has the following accolades.
- He was named a Vice President of the USATT.
- He was an original member of the USATT Ping Pong Diplomacy team to the People's Republic of China.
- He was a USATT Certified National Table Tennis Coach.

- He is an inductee into the USA Table Tennis Hall of Fame.
- He has received the USATT Lifetime Achievement Award.
- He has represented the USA at the World's Table Tennis Championship.
- He has represented the USA at the Pan American Games.
- He was selected as a member of the US team to the World's Table Tennis Championship in Nagoya, Japan, for which he was featured on the cover of the April 26, 1971, issue of Time magazine.

Sadly, October 29, 2020, the table tennis community lost a friend. George Brathwaite died at eighty-six of COVID-19.

An original member of the 1971 Ping Pong Diplomacy team, George was known affectionately as "The Chief." I knew him as my friend and doubles partner. I am deeply saddened by his passing. RIP, George. God bless you.

George was an inspiration for me—his lifestyle, his work ethic, his commitment to the sport—and he motivated me to work harder, especially during the many doubles matches we played together.

Me & my O80 doubles partner and friend George Braithwaite competing in the WVC2018 in Las Vegas, June 19, 2018. Photo by Mal Anderson.

GEORGE HENDRY

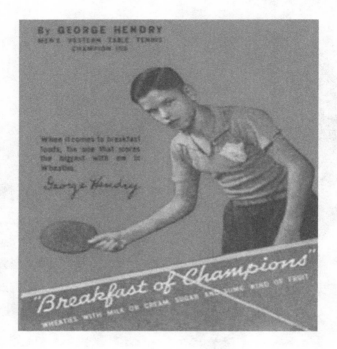

GEORGE HENDRY WON his first National Junior Table Tennis Championship in 1935 at age fourteen, becoming the number one rated American player in doubles and number two in singles, the best player in the world pushed to the brink of defeat, and later chosen to appear on the *Wheaties* box.

The sport's popularity in 1935 was such that its stars, young Hendry included, barnstormed the nation, appearing in places like Radio City Music Hall with vaudeville stars and bandleaders like Benny Goodman, whacking trick shots for thousands of spectators at a time.

George Hendry and me
US Nationals, 2009

Then, in 1952, Hendry decided to quit table tennis to devote himself to building his accounting business in his native St. Louis and to spend time with his family. He stopped playing for over two decades.

But in 1976 he started playing—in the senior circuit. The press referred to George Hendry as "the comeback kid."

It wasn't easy. Table tennis had changed; a layer of sponge had been added underneath the regulation rubber-covered paddle, making the game much faster.

He ultimately won thirty-five national seniors championships.

In 1990, he won the world championship for players over seventy. He won his last National Championship at eighty-nine in the over-eighty group.

George's legendry status in the sport of table tennis was assured. In the seventy-five-year span of his career—his number of winning National titles starting in 1914 and moving all the way into the 1980s—he rivaled the careers of contemporaries like Sol Schiff, Lou Pagliaro, Dick Miles, and Marty Reisman.

KEN LEES

ON AUGUST 7, 2009, I received a call from a table tennis friend named Hiep Tran, asking if I would come to a 4:00 P.M. meeting at Starbucks on Virginia Beach Boulevard. When I asked him what the meeting was about, he said, "It has something to do with ping-pong."

The meeting was run by a fellow named Ken Lees to discuss the possibility of employing the game of ping-pong as a method of fundraising. The first Ping-Pong for Poverty charity tournament, held just six weeks later on September 19, 2009, at Courthouse Community United Methodist Church's Family Life Center, raised $13,000 for people in need. Ping Pong for Poverty has evolved into the Table Tennis Charity Foundation which is committed to raising awareness of the therapeutic value that playing table tennis offers for mental health and brain fitness.

The vision of the foundation is also to integrate sports and education table tennis programs with senior living communities, rehabilitation/medical facilities, and the Virginia Beach school system. The foundation also stresses utilizing the brain-stimulating sport of table tennis to raise money for charity partners who directly benefit those facing Alzheimer's, dementia, depression, and Parkinson's Disease.

Over the years, charity events have featured table tennis exhibitions performed by some of the most skilled exhibition players in the country—Scott and Austin Preiss, Wally Green and Kazuyuki (Kaz) Yokoyama, Ioana Papadimitriou, and basketball legend Christian Laettner.

For a basketball legend, Christian Laettner is an amazing table tennis player.

2016 was our eighth year working with the founder of the charity, Ken Lees. This year, we raised $55,000, for a total of nearly $500,000 raised for participating charities.

My role, along with Ken and Dr. Scott Sautter in this very worthwhile charity, which is now to serve as a member of the Board of Directors, started by "just showing up" at a Starbucks in August 2009 to attend a meeting about which I knew little other than it was "about ping-pong," but which has become one of the most *divinely inspired* events of my lifetime.

March 18, 2016, I received an email from the Eastern Virginia Medical School.

It read:

> "*Date is Wednesday March 30.*
> "*Six residents from Harbor's Edge retirement community are going to visit our campus, arriving at 11:50 A.M. They will be ready to play some serious ping-pong with Eastern Virginia Medical School students. The event is being sponsored by the Psychiatry Interest Group and the Neurology Interest Group at the Eastern Virginia Medical School in Norfolk.*
> "*The event is called a 'Brain Fitness and ping-pong presentation by Neuropsychologist Dr. Scott Sautter, and table tennis player Dean Johnson.'*"

DR. SCOTT SAUTTER,
DR. PAUL ARAVICH

Dr. Scott Sautter

My role in the event was to hit a few balls and give some tips to both students and residents of Harbor's Edge. It was all good—all fun.

During the event, Dr. Sautter introduced me to Dr. Paul Aravich, who was apparently in attendance mainly to observe the proceedings, especially the presentation by Dr. Sautter. I later learned that Dr. Aravich is a behavioral neuroscientist and professor of pathology and anatomy, geriatrics, and physical medicine and rehabilitation at EVMS.

Dr. Aravich and I made some small talk, which included a question about my age. When I told him I was eighty-six, his mouth literally dropped open. He then told me that he was conducting a seminar on dementia care that afternoon and asked if I would be interested in attending. Following my theory of "just show up," I said that I would be there. He said the seminar would be just down the hall and asked me to be at the entrance to the auditorium at 2:30.

Since it was now just 1:30, I helped myself to some lunch which was provided by the school. There was still another thirty minutes before I had to head to the auditorium, so I went back to the student lounge to relax.

Three students arrived at the lounge about the time I did, and I overheard them talk about wanting to play some ping-pong doubles, but they needed a fourth, so I volunteered.

What ensued for the next thirty minutes may have been some of the most entertaining doubles I've ever played.

The students were, of course, recreational-level players.

I decided, as I usually do, to keep my play at a recreational level, unless, in the interest of my partner, we needed a point or two in a close game; even then, I kept my returns subtle. To under-spin or soft top-spin confused both of our opponents, but it also caused them to start giggling.

After losing several games in a row, our opponents just could not understand why it was not possible for them to win even one game! In desperation, one of them unleashed one of the hardest flat forehands you can imagine—as if coming from a professional player. The ball bounced off the table and struck my bat, which happened to be angled perfectly for a block and which caused the ball to ricochet to the white line on their side of the table. The two of them began laughing so hard we could not resume play for several minutes!

The three students persuaded me to stay on the table until it was precisely time for me to head to the auditorium. As I was leaving, I said, "I've played some table tennis in my life. In fact, I was recently inducted into the US Table Tennis Hall of Fame." More laughter from the students. As I left the student lounge, I overheard one of them say, "I knew there was something weird about the way that guy played."

When I arrived at the entrance to the auditorium, I found nine women waiting to enter. After I filled out some disclaimer forms, one of them motioned for me to come with her. Her name was Amy, and she led my way to a table on the stage where eleven seats had been placed with a microphone and a bottle of water for each!

What Dr. Aravich did not tell me was that he was not just expecting me to "attend" his seminar but to sit on a panel with ten "experts" on the treatment of Alzheimer's and dementia and to make a presentation on the subject to 200 medical students who were just now beginning to file into the auditorium!

I only learned, officially, what my role was to be when Dr. Aravich announced from the podium that, "We have a special guest with us today. His name is Dean Johnson. He's a member of the Table Tennis Hall of Fame and he'll speak to us about some of the positive effects that table tennis may have on the prevention and treatment of dementia. He'll be our first speaker." By this time, realizing that I was not prepared to speak, I was in full panic mode.

With nowhere to hide short of saying to Dr. Aravich, "I wasn't aware that you invited me to speak, I'm sorry, I'm not prepared,"

I had to quickly come up with something meaningful to say to the students. By some miracle, my thoughts raced to what Dr. Sautter had to say that morning about the benefits that table tennis has on "brain function and brain fitness."

I had to start somewhere, so I said, "Table tennis is truly a game for life. I'm eighty-six. While table tennis may be only a part of the reason for my apparent good health, I think it has been an important part. I've played competitive table tennis or tennis for nearly sixty years, and I can't think of any other aspect of my lifestyle that may have contributed to my good health at this stage of my life as much as racket sports has. Dr. Sautter, in his presentation this morning, spoke about the benefits of 'cross-training your brain,' with aerobic exercise, by solving mental problems, and by establishing social connections and relationships. Participating in the sport of table tennis has done all of that for me. And I believe that 'cross-training' your brain can benefit anyone, at any age, at any stage of one's life.

Dr. Paul Aravich & Me

"Physical exercise is an obvious benefit to playing table tennis, even at a recreational level. Table tennis has an 'addictive' quality to it. You cannot play just one game of table tennis; it's always 'let's play one more.' Problem solving is also a challenge for table tennis players. Opponents are continually throwing up challenges and questions: here's a ball with under-spin, what will you do with it? Here's a dead ball with no spin, what will you do with it? As a table tennis player, your brain must constantly work to solve a variety of strategic problems.

"The opportunities for social interaction and establishing relationships through table tennis are without limit. I still have friends whom I met through table tennis more than sixty years ago—including my best friend, my wife, whom I met at a table tennis tournament in 1962 and to whom I've been married for fifty-five years.

"A recent eleven-year study showed that of all the factors known to contribute to longevity, such as diet, exercise, and healthy social interaction, true friendships, in a wide variety of ways, has a crucial role in increasing not just the length but the quality of lives of older people.

"Dr. Sautter also made us aware this morning of something I never knew which is the concept of 'neuroplasticity'—the proven theory that the brain can physically change in response to repeated intense activity, such as correctly and repeatedly executing a table tennis stroke. The old adage 'practice makes perfect' is not completely true; 'perfect practice makes perfect' is more accurate. With the knowledge that your brain can physically change with perfect practice comes the knowledge that you are not bound by old, bad habits; it means that you can always improve, which, in turn, means there is no limit to how advanced you can become in the sport."

These thoughts led me to recall things I had heard recently about the importance of *balance* in life, which I shared with the students. "While table tennis has filled for me at least three of the pieces in the complex puzzle that makes for a balanced life—aerobic fitness, brain fitness, and social interaction—they're not the only ingredients important in walking the tight rope called a 'balanced life.' Balance in one's family life is important (keep your family close). Spiritual balance is important (whether you believe in God or not, He's with you at all times. However, I believe that without God, life has no purpose, and without purpose, life has no meaning). Find purpose in your work. Find what you love to do; if you can do that, you won't work a day in your life.

"All of these ingredients are not easy to acquire, but they're achievable; all are worth seeking, because, combined, they can lead to the formula for a long and happy life."

Nine more presentations by the panel followed, after which our panel received a standing ovation from the students. Out of the crowd, I saw my doubles partner from the afternoon heading toward the stage with a paddle in his hand. He brought it for me to autograph!

On September 28th, 2016, a phone call came in from Doug Gardner, head of Marketing Communications and editor of a magazine published by the Eastern Virginia Medical School. He had heard about my appearance on the dementia panel. He wanted to request an interview for an article he would like to do on my table tennis career and on how table tennis may have contributed to my apparently healthy condition at my age.

I agreed, and we scheduled a meeting with Doug and his videographer, Jessie Wilde, at Bayside Recreation Center at 2:30 on October 4th. The meeting included a video interview, a hitting session, and still photos of me playing.

When Doug and Jessie arrived at the rec center, which had graciously supplied us with a private room for the interview and a table for hitting, I was very impressed by the amount of equipment they brought in—a video camera, two still cameras, five lights on tripods, and sound equipment. The room began to look like a photo/TV studio.

Once everything was set up in the room, the interview segment took about thirty minutes. We arrived in the lobby about 3:15, where my hitting partner, Tom, was waiting.

My prior experience with photo shoots of my hitting was that they usually took no more than fifteen or twenty minutes. Doug and Jessie started shooting exactly at 3:30. At 4:50, they were still shooting!

Except for one bathroom break, it was non-stop forehands and backhands. I was stroking the ball while Tom was blocking— hitting softly enough just to keep the ball in play while Doug and Jessie were filming. Most of the rallies of forehands and backhands were twenty or thirty times over the net so Doug and Jessie could get the action shots they needed.

I estimated that I stroked the ball 2,200 times! I slept well that night.

I have found it fascinating in my life how a "just show up" fun event that began on March 18 can evolve six months later into what was for me a *divinely inspired*, life-altering experience.

IONNA PAPADIMITRIOU

FOR THREE CONSECUTIVE years, Ioanna was Greek National Table Tennis Champion. She trained with the Greek National Selects team and represented Greece in several international tournaments.

In 1994, Ioanna was crowned Miss Greece which signaled the beginning of a modeling career for her and led to being known as a "World Class Super Model."

Ioanna's yearly exhibitions at PingPong.Gives Charity Foundation events have made an enormous contribution to their success.

(She also very graciously offered to help me promote my latest book: *A Table For Two*.)

ADONI MAROPIS

THANKS LARGELY TO Adoni's celebrity, the 2011 US Nationals made the front page of the Virginian-Pilot. During an interview with Virginia Beach TV's Bill Casey, Adoni was asked why he traveled all the way from California to compete in this event. He replied, "To show support for my friend, Dean Johnson." Adoni was pleased with the fact that the action photo in *The Pilot* shows me standing in the background. He said it symbolized to him the "looking after" that Helga and I provided for him while he was here.

Adonis' imdb page, https://www.imdb.com/nA.M.e/nm0549538/bio, highlights his biography.

Being an exceptional athlete in . . . high school . . . it appeared that Adoni would pursue a professional career in some sport. Turning down various athletic scholarships . . . he transferred to West Virginia University . . . [and] graduated magna cum laude But . . . his father ,Petro, told him that the suit and tie of the business world would probably choke him to death. . . . [he] took off for Hollywood.

. . . Adoni has [since] been blessed with the opportunity to play many diverse and memorable acting roles, such as the lead villain, Fayed, in season six of the Fox critically acclaimed hit series 24 with Kiefer Sutherland.

. . . Although, Adoni has been blessed with creative talent, what truly makes Adonis stand-out is that he is a Type 1 Diabetic and has been since he was 18 months old. His parents were told he would be weak, sick, and in and out of hospitals throughout his life. Ultimately, a renowned diabetic specialist told his father that most likely Adonis would be dead by the age of 25. Of course, Adonis has long past the age of 25, and he credits 3 things for his success in life: Love, laughter, and Fitness!

This was Adoni's inscription in my book, *A Table For Two*:

Dean, you and Helga were amazing hosts and surrogate parents to me at the 2011 Nationals. I believe the two of you are a big part of the reason I won the Hardbat Championship. The picture on the cover of the Pilot is such a perfect photo, because it represents to me my father and my guru coach, Carlos, who could be you in the picture. Congratulations on the book and on your amazing life.

—Adoni

Adoni & Me. US Nationals June 22, 2018, Las Vegas.

DAVID SAKAI / DAN SEEMILLER

JANUARY 17TH, 2014, in a call from friend David Sakai—winner of every National Senior Singles and Doubles title, over thirty, forty, fifty, sixty, and sixty-five since 1984—he shares with me the fact that he and Danny Seemiller (five-time US Singles Champion) are planning to submit a bid to bring the 2018 WVC (World Veteran Championships) to Las Vegas.

I was pleased to hear from David but not quite sure why he was calling me. In hindsight, perhaps it had to do with my role as Chairman of the 2011 US Nationals Local Organizing Committee, which brought the US Nationals to Virginia Beach—the first time it was held in a city other than Las Vegas in thirty years.

What was also not clear to me at the time was the business relationship between David and Danny and the USATT in this process.

In a casual meeting with Danny at the 2014 US Nationals, he shared with me that he had discussions with Gordon Kaye, recently appointed USATT CEO, and that he and David agreed with Gordon that the bid should be organized by USATT and that Senoda (David's company) would be a major sponsor.

So, for a time, the Local Organizing Committee for 2018 WVC was me, David, and Danny.

By the end of December 2014, however, through a series of e-mails from Gordon Kaye, it became clear that Gordon and the USATT would take the lead in the bidding process.

At a meeting between the Swathling Club Committee (organizers of WVC) and members of the USATT Local Organizing Committee (Gordon, David, and Danny) during the WVC 2016 in Alicante, Spain, I learned of the news that an agreement between the USATT, David, and Danny had been reached and signed.

Photo of David courtesy Joola

This was good news and somewhat of a relief to me, because, from my experience with the 2011 Nationals, I saw how overwhelming it could be for anything less than an organization the size of the USATT to take on such a monumental project. And when the bid specifications began to come in from Gloria Wagener at SCI (Swathling Club International), I could see the tasks were considerable—even for the USATT.

But Gordon took on this historic challenge—not only willingly, but with a passion. David, Danny, and I supported him in every way possible, preparing the detailed application to bid and the PowerPoint presentation to be made to the WVC Committee during the World Table Tennis Championships in Suzhou, China.

I shot a video during the actual announcement by Hans Westling, Chairman of the WVC Committee, when, on April 27, 2015, WVC 2018 was awarded to Las Vegas. Check that video out here: https://vimeo.com/126744495.

The final Local Organizing Committee WVC 2018 consisted of Gordon Kaye, Danny Seemiller, Stellan Bengtsson, Mike Babuin, David Sakai, and me. Presentations in Suzhou were made by Gordon, Mike, and me. My involvement in the WVC 2018 bidding process can be traced back to Mike Babuin's call to me on October 18, 2010, alerting me to the fact that Virginia Beach had submitted a bid to host the 2011 US Nationals.

I was subsequently named Chairman of the 2011 Local Organizing Committee and led the team to a highly successful event, which, in turn, I believe, led to David Sakai's call to me in January 2014 to join him and Danny Seemiller in an effort to submit a bid for WVC 2018—and even further back than that, on a linked chain to the *divinely inspired* event on August 20, 1956, when a coin fell in Jan Carlsson's favor on a street on the outskirts of Nice, France!

USA Table Tennis presenters in Suzhou, China—USATT
CEO Gordon Kaye, me, and Mike Babuin, posing with Hans
Westling, Chairman of the WVC Committee, who announced
the decision that Las Vegas will be the organizer for WVC
2018.

HANS WESTLING

CONTINUING THE PREVIOUS story about how a call from David Sakai in January 2014 resulted in my involvement in the 2018 WVC (World Veterans Championships), during the process, a friendship developed between me and Hans Westling, Chairman of the WVC Committee. It did not take long for us to realize that we had much in common—not only a Swedish connection, but through Hans' many years of involvement in World Veterans Championships, he was very familiar with my father-in-law, Heinrich Bültemeier, who was a frequent participant in World Veterans Championships events.

In many casual conversations that Hans and I had about the preparation of the bid for the record-breaking World Veteran

Championship, it was clear to me that he believed strongly in emphasizing Las Vegas in the bid presentation.

Hans Westling arranged for a press release to be placed in the March 2016 (100th) edition of Swathling Club magazine, announcing my induction into the US Table Tennis Hall of Fame.

JOHN KOEHLER

TAKEN FROM THE Koehler Books Team website, <u>https://www.koehlerbooks.com/about/our-team/</u>, John's bio states:

> John is the company founder and runs its day-to-day operations. He is an award-winning graphics designer, and the author of seven books. He was awarded the lifetime achievement Silver Medal by the Advertising Federation of Hampton Roads in 2016. He earned a BFA in Communications Arts and Design from Virginia Commonwealth University and attended graduate studies at George Washington University in Washington, D.C. John's professional career includes being senior art director of a major advertising agency

and running a design studio. John lives in Virginia Beach, VA and is active in his church. He has helped run a ministry dedicated to helping children with disabilities, a cause he is still very much dedicated to. John made an international splash in 1991 by winning the Boomerang World Championship in Perth, Australia and was a member of the Foster's Boomerang 2000 Team, a touring troop that taught professional athletes, and others, the gospel of boomerangs.

SCI PRESS RELEASE

THE FOLLOWING SECTION is written by Hans Wrestling, found on http://archive.constantcontact.com/ fs170/1102964308314/archive/1123380215969.html, in the USA Table Tennis Insider.

Member of the Swaythling Club International and ITTF Veteran Committee member, Dean Johnson was inducted into the USTTA Hall of Fame [on December 17, 2015].

The presentation was made during the United States National Championships held in Las Vegas, Nevada on Thursday 17th December; attending the occasion was Sweden's Hans Westling, Chair of the World Veteran Championships Committee. Notably, in 2018 Las Vegas will host the World Veteran Championship; Dean Johnson is a member of the Organizing Committee.

Entitled: "The United States Table Tennis Hall of Fame." The citation reads, "Dean Johnson, whose outstanding service and contributions to the sport of table tennis have earned him worldwide recognition and admiration in its finest tradition."

Current Roles: Currently, Dean Johnson is Chair of the United States Hall of Fame Museum located at the Triangle Table Tennis Club in Morrisville, North Carolina.

Additionally, Dean is a founding member and presently on the Board of Directors of the Table Tennis Charity Foundation which, over a period of seven years, has raised a total of $323,000 for charities and people in need.

Third Time: Furthermore, it was not the only accolade that Dean Johnson secured at the United States National Championships. Partnering with George Brathwaite, the duo won their third Men's Doubles over-eighty title.

USA Table Tennis presenters in Suzhou, China, World Veteran Championships Committee with USATT Local Organizing Committee: (standing) Mike Babuin, Reto Bazzi, Gordon Kaye, me, Michael Theis. (Seated) Werner Schnyder, Diane Schöler, Eberhard Schöler, Gloria Wagener, and Hans Westling.

DEAN'S USTTA HALL OF FAME ACCEPTANCE SPEECH

(edited for clarity)

THANK YOU, TIM.

It's with a great deal of humility that I accept and thank our Hall of Fame Committee for inducting me into the US Table Tennis Hall of Fame.

Also, I'd like to give a special thanks to our CEO Gordon Kaye for securing this wonderful facility in which to hold our dinner here tonight. And also, by the way, for Gordon's leadership and skill in guiding us to a successful bid for WVC 2018. Our membership is very fortunate to have you, Gordon, as our CEO.

Also, a shout-out to Mike Babuin for his support and help in establishing our Hall of Fame Museum at Triangle Table Tennis in Morrisville, North Carolina.

Being in the right place at the right time is often not only the key to success in life but often determines the path of one's entire life.

Good fortune and divine guidance have played an enormous role in my life.

I was in the right place at the right time when, in 1957, I came across a little $1.25 book by Coleman Clark in a Barnes and Noble in Manhattan that would bring me to this place at this time fifty-eight years later.

This is the book. $1.25 changed my life.

In his book, Clark profiled world-class American players of the day—Sol Schiff, Dick Miles, Jimmy McClure, Lou Pagliaro, Marty Reisman, Ruth Aarons, and Sally Green Prouty.

Of these future American legends of the game, many of them lived and practiced in New York. I was immediately bound and determined to find out where.

Just a recreational-level basement player, I was eager to see firsthand what world-class table tennis looked like.

A search the following afternoon in the fall of 1957 lead me to the corner of Broadway and 96th Street in Manhattan, a few steps below street level.

Rather than finding a hot bed of table tennis I had expected, the place was dark except for a bare bulb above a desk to the left of the entrance at which sat a thirty-something-year-old man to whom I said, "Hi, my name is Dean. Is this the place where the good players play?" He never answered my question. Instead, he just said: "You want to play?"

I said, "No thanks, I just want to see good players play."

"I Bernie Bukiet," he said. "I your national champion. You have big country here. How come you can't find someone beat me?" (I learned later that Bernie had just won the Men's Singles in South Bend, Indiana.)

I ended up staying until nearly dawn the next day, watching Miles, Reisman, Bukiet, Cartland, Bobby Gusikoff, Leah Neuberger, and Pauline Somael battle in the most amazing display of table tennis I had ever seen. I was hooked!

Table tennis, with just 2,500 registered players at the time, was really a sub-culture compared to sports like baseball, football, and basketball. I was so excited by what I had seen. I remember wondering at the time, *if I worked really hard, could I be somebody in this game?*

This night turned out to be life-altering for me. It began an incredible adventure which brought me together with Helga, whom I met at the Canadian Nationals in 1962, brought three beautiful children into the world, and introduced me to the great sport of table tennis, to a wonderful group of people, many of whom have become close friends.

Incredibly, in addition, nearly every business client I had after the late 1960s was directly or indirectly connected to table tennis—and that continued for more than forty years.

One of my proudest achievements is the six-volume history set covering 1931-1966 that I compiled over ten years. This was a period in which an American woman won two worlds' singles championships, three American men won three worlds' doubles championships, two American women and two American men won two worlds' mixed doubles championship, three American men advanced to the semi-finals in world championships, and one American teenager was the youngest ever to win a US open championship. This period in our history should not be forgotten.

I use the word "compiled" here, in putting this set together, because most of the credit for this series goes to my friend Tim Boggan—for the records he kept, for the writing he did—and to Mal Anderson and his photographs which preserve the history of our sport. They have both contributed mightily to this unique period in American table tennis history, and they continue to contribute. My contribution was only to do the things I love in bringing it all together in published form—which is what I did in my career.

My plan now, in "semi" retirement, is to continue to promote events for veteran players nationwide and to continue to promote the health benefits of our sport. Especially to senior citizens, physical fitness and brain fitness, along with a healthy lifestyle, has clinically proven that regular participation in table tennis promotes a more balanced and happier life.

As you have seen, table tennis has had a profound impact on

my life for nearly sixty years. I have our great sport to thank for all I have, and I have you to thank, my friends here, for making this such a wonderful evening for me. And I share it, as I have my life for fifty-three years, with my dear wife Helga.

It is a joy and a privilege for me to again be at the right place at the right time in my life to receive this honor tonight.

You have all made me very proud. I'm honored, beyond words, to receive this award. I'm deeply honored to be in the company of other Hall of Fame contributors and officials and to even be mentioned in the same breath with Hall of Fame Players.

Thank you.

As I stepped off the stage, I wondered to myself, *have I become somebody in this sport that I love?* I don't know the answer to that, but I believe I've made more of an impression than I ever imagined I would. I have no doubt that this honor given to me was *divinely inspired*! These stories are about THEM, and as it turns out, they're a little about me, too.

LIFE'S LESSONS LEARNED

DO THE THINGS you love, and you'll never work a day in your life. Actress Betty White, who turned ninety-six four days before I turned eighty-six, agrees. She says she loves to work. "I'll stop working when they stop asking," she says. (She calls what she does "work," but she loves what she does.)

Confidence morphing into overconfidence, humility morphing into arrogance, is a formula for failure.

Develop good daily habits; they'll work for you every day.

Longevity is connected to balance—balance in one's family life, one's social life, one's working life, one's spiritual life, financial life, diet, and physical fitness. It's a delicate balance that requires discipline. Having all of them in your life offers no guarantee to longevity, but maintaining balance greatly improves one's chances for a long and happy life.

A recent study showed that, of all the factors known to contribute to longevity such as diet, exercise, and healthy social interaction, true friendships and social interactions ranked the highest.

To achieve something—this evening, plan your work; tomorrow morning—start working your plan.

My friend, Bill Lechler, had a great sense of humor. First thing every morning, he would manage to start the day with something humorous for his team. One of my favorites was, "Three things to remember, men, as you get older: Never pass up a bathroom, never waste an erection, and never trust a fart."

Without God, life has no purpose. Without purpose, life has no meaning.

Nearly every man to whom I reported in my career is gone. I loved each of them, but they all suffered, I believe, either from a disproportionate focus on symbolism or, in retirement, the devastating effects of a loss of mission and purpose in their lives.

Coincidence is God's way of remaining anonymous.

ACKNOWLEDGMENTS

I WAS GUIDED on my path by my mother Helen Donohue Johnson and my grandmother Anna Marie Warloe Johnson, who, by their example, were spiritual beacons and inspirations; also, by my uncle John Donohue, who loved me and showed it when he gave me a stern lecture when he heard from my mother that I planned to quit high school at sixteen, to uncle Victor Johnson who devoted much of his time to me when his brother Dean was an absentee father, by Erika and Heinrich Bültemeier who so lovingly, graciously, unconditionally, and immediately accepted me, a foreigner from America, into their home and into their family.

I'm also grateful for all of those who have called me their friend—e.g. the greatest table tennis players of the forties, fifties, and sixties—Dick Miles, Marty Reisman, Lou Pagliaro, and Sol Schiff, to the greatest player in the history of college basketball, Christian Laettner, to Maestro Dexter Grey who has mastered the piano like no other performer of his genre, to Harold Evans voted by *Inside Story*'s Davis Hayes as the "most esteemed British newspaper editor of the twentieth century," to Frank Brennan Jr., among other honors named PAC-12 Women's College Tennis Coach of the Century, to my most recent friend, John Koehler, a highly successful publisher and 1991 World Boomerang Champion, to Ioanna Papadimitriou three-time Greek National Table Tennis Champion, crowned Miss Greece in 1994 and enormous contributor to Ping Pong for Charity, to

Jack Brady who, despite his treacherous and ruthless nature, led the way to my first employment at Kniep's advertising agency, to Louis Kniep who brought me not only into his business but treated me like a son, to Phillip Graham Vance and Jan Carlsson, faithful friends for nearly seventy years, to Peter Renzo, who not only brought me into Sier-Bath but accepted me as a member of the Sier-Bath family, to Hans Westling, who, with his knowledge of the World Veterans Championships, helped guide me and the WVC committee through the complex network of paths that we had to negotiate in order to bring the tournament to Las Vegas and the largest table tennis event ever held, to Bill Lechler, who not only brought me into Sumitomo as an ad agent but "had my back" during the turbulent '90s and paved the way for me to be a Sumitomo employee by acquiring our business and facilitating our relocation to Virginia Beach, to Greg Jordan, who, along with his father Deck, on a day in 1988, demonstrated a faith in me that turned a potential disaster for me into a thirteen-year highly successful business and personal relationship.

Most importantly, to my wife, my inspiration, Helga Renate Bültemeier Johnson who had the faith to take a chance on me and has put up with me for fifty-seven years.

I did my best to care for others, but they cared for me more.

Today, many of those who helped bring me to where I am are gone, but I continue to be guided by my Heavenly Father—by the divine intelligence that I believe permeates the universe, which is as real to me as my earthly guides. All of them appeared in my life at precisely the right time and led me to this time and place in my life.

"You put the words together,
and you hope they're in the right order.
If they are, perhaps you gave the world a nudge."
—Unknown

Soul Helper
"An individual who comes into your life for a moment,
lifetime, or anywhere in between and helps you soul move
toward growth, healing, and alignment."
—Morris Jackson,
a dear friend, a quote found on his Facebook page

Grateful acknowledgement is made for images on the following pages:
Page 121: Photo by Mal Anderson
Page 148: David Sakai Joola photo Page 152: ITTF photo
All other images courtesy of the author

ADDENDUM—BILL WESTBROOK

ME AND NINETY-NINE-YEAR young Bill Westbrook at The Crossings of Harborview—a retirement community in Suffolk, Virginia. After I hit a few with Bill, I told him that he was now his new role model.

ADDENDUM—JAN CARLSSON

THIS GIFT CALLED "Lyftet" was created especially for me by a famous Swedish sculptor, given to me by Jan during his visit in 1956. "Lyftet" is the Swedish term for "The Lift," and in this case, refers to the many struggles Jan has carried with him during his lifetime.

BIBLIOGRAPHY AND REFERENCES

Read About the Ones Who've Inspired Me

"Adoni Maropis." IMDb. IMDb.com. Accessed December 14, 2021. https://www.imdb.com/name/nm0549538/bio.

"Hall of Fame Committee." Team USA. Accessed December 14, 2021. https://www.teamusa.org/USA-Table-Tennis/History/Hall-of-Fame/Committee.

"History." George Braithwaite. Accessed December 14, 2021. https://www.georgebraithwaite.com/about/.

Kennedy, Ray. "A Little Night Music - Sports Illustrated Vault." SI.com. Sports Illustrated Vault | SI.com, November 21, 1977. https://vault.si.com/vault/1977/11/21/a-little-night-music.

Marty Reisman: A Retrospective, Volume I

Medenilla, Klarize, Momar G. Visaya, Asian Journal Press, Ritchel Mendiola, Contributor, AD Supports, Jason Agcaoili, et al. "Dexter Grey: Rebellious Audacity and Improvisations Highlight Latest Concert -." Asian Journal News, February 21, 2018. https://www.asianjournal.com/life-style/dexter-grey-rebellious-audacity-and-improvisations-highlight-latest-concert/.

Mylah De Leon, "Dexter Grey: Rebellious Audacity And Improvisations Highlight Latest Concert," *Asian*

Journal, August 13, 2016.

"Our Team." Koehler Books Publishing. Accessed December 14, 2021. https://www.koehlerbooks.com/about/our-team/.

"USA Table Tennis Hall of Fame Profile - Angelita Rosal Bengtsson." Team USA. Accessed December 14, 2021. https://www.teamusa.org/USA-Table-Tennis/History/Hall-of-Fame/Profiles/Angelita-Rosal-Bengtsson.

"USA Table Tennis Hall of Fame Profile - Erwin Klein." Team USA. Accessed December 14, 2021. https://www.teamusa.org/USA-Table-Tennis/History/Hall-of-Fame/Profiles/Erwin-Klein.

"USA Table Tennis Hall of Fame Profile - Norbert Van De Walle." Team USA. Accessed December 14, 2021. https://www.teamusa.org/USA-Table-Tennis/History/Hall-of-Fame/Profiles/Norbert-Van-de-Walle.

USATT insider - January 6, 2016. Accessed December 14, 2021. http://archive.constantcontact.com/fs170/1102964308314/archive/1123380215969.html.

Weber, Bruce. "Dick Miles, Record-Setting U.S. Table Tennis Player, Dies at 85." *The New York Times*, October 23, 2010. https://www.nytimes.com/2010/10/24/sports/24miles.html.